THE CHURCH VIEWED FROM THE PALACE GREEN, AND THE EAST.

Historical Sketch of Bruton Church

Williamsburg, Virginia.

By

Revd. W. A. R. Goodwin, A. M.

Rector of Bruton Church

CLEARFIELD

Originally published
Petersburg, Virginia, 1903

Reprinted for
Clearfield Company, Inc. by
Genealogical Publishing Co., Inc.
Baltimore, Maryland
1995, 1997

International Standard Book Number: 0-8063-4600-0

Made in the United States of America

Dedication

To

The Congregation of Old Bruton Church, and to Those who will share with them in the privilege of Restoring and Preserving this ancient Temple of our fore-fathers, this work is affectionately dedicated.

Preface

THIS historical sketch has been compiled in order to supply the constant demand for information as to the early history of Old Bruton Church. The information given is largely derived from an article on the history of Bruton Church written by Rev. Jno. C. McCabe, and published in the Church Review, January, 1856. Dr. McCabe had the use of the old vestry book of the Parish containing the records of the Church from 1674 to 1769. Extensive and interesting extracts from this book were copied by him, and an endeavor has been made to embody every one of those in this sketch for reference and preservation, as the book from which they were copied never came again into the possession of the Vestry. They are printed in Old English type. Use has also been made of Bishop Meade's "Old Churches and Families in Virginia," and of a sketch of Bruton Church written by President Lyon G. Tyler, of the College of William and Mary. We have also referred to Hening's Early Statutes of Va., and to Vol 1 of Calendar of State Papers 1652-1781, and made use of the subsequent records of the Parish. The tablets on the walls of the Church have been copied and inserted, and also some of the most interesting inscriptions on the tombstones in the Church and Church-yard, and the names contained in the Birth and Death record of the Old Parish Register of 1662 have been inserted.

With grateful appreciation I acknowledge the kindness of the Rev. F. G. Scott, of the Bishop Payne Divinity School, Petersburg, Va., through whose hands the proof-sheets of this work have passed.

W. A. R. G.

BRUTON RECTORY,
    WILLIAMSBURG, VA.,
        Feast of the Transfiguration, 1903.

Contents

	PAGE
Historical Associations,	7
History of the Formation of the Parish,	11
Old Records Relating to the Building of 1683,	12
Death of Rev. Rowland Jones, and Election of Rev. James Sclater,	17
Election of Rev. Samuel Eburne,	17
A Silver Service Given,	18
Rev. Cope Doyley Elected,	20
Removal of the Seat of Government from Jamestown to Williamsburg,	20
Election of Rev. Solomon Wheatley,	22
Conflict as to Right of Induction,	23
Position and Authority of Colonial Vestrymen,	24
Election of Commissary Blair, Minister,	27
The Church of 1715,	31
Election of Rev. Thomas Dawson,	37
The Church Enlarged and Organ Secured,	37
The Church-yard Wall,	39
The Belfry Built,	39
Some Old Vestry Orders,	41
The Passing of the Old Regime,	45
The Church after the Revolution, Legislative Despoliation,	49
Early Episcopal Visitations,	51
Dr. Bracken, Dr. Keith, Dr. Wilmer, Dr. Empie, Rectors,	51–54
Modern Innovations,	55
The Colonial Governor's Pew, The Mayor's Pew,	57
The List of Pew Holders in 1840,	59
The Clock in the Steeple,	60
The Restoration Movement,	63
The Old Communion Silver, Font, Old Bell, Old Parish Register,	68–72
Extracts from Sermons of Commissary Blair,	72
Induction Controversy,	Appendix A
Mural Tablets and Tombstone Inscriptions,	Appendix B
The Ministers and Vestrymen of Bruton Parish,	Appendix C
Birth Record,	Appendix D
Death Record,	Appendix E

Illustrations

1. The Church seen from the Palace Green and the East, - - - - - Frontispiece
2. Colonial view of the Church, - - - - 14
3. The Old Tower at Jamestown, - - - - 21
4. Portrait of Commissary Blair, . - - - 27
5. The Jamestown Font, - - - - - 30
6. The Silver-Gold Service, called the "Queen Anne Set," - - - - - - - - - 30
7. The Church seen from the Church-yard, - - 41
8. The Church viewed from the Duke of Gloucester Street, - - - - - - - - 48
9. Interior view of the Church, 1840-1886, - - 57
10. The Duke of Gloucester Street, - - - - 57
11. Diagram showing the Original and Present Arrangement of the Church, - - - - 58
12. Interior view of the Church, 1886-1903, - - 62
13. The Jamestown Communion Service, - - 68
14. The King George Communion Service, - - 70
15. The Church Yard - - - - - - - 87
16. Two Pages of the Old Parish Register, Appendix D

Associations

OLD Bruton Church has well withstood the devastating touch of time. The storms of many winters have gone over it, the fierce battles of two great wars have raged near it, and in it have lain the sick and wounded of two armies, and yet it stands to-day just as it stood well nigh two hundred years ago. The Building is consecrated by hallowed associations. It is intimately connected with Virginia's early history. Through its ancient tower entrance passed the Court processions of Colonial days,— the governors with emblazoned emblems, betokening the authority and majesty of old England's Kings and Queens; the Council of State, composed of men whose names will ever live in our nation's history; and the members of the House of Burgesses, the defenders of the liberties of the people.

Here, in pew officially assigned, elevated from the main floor and richly canopied, sat the proud and imperious Francis Nicholson, the devoted Edmund Jennings, the dauntless Spottswood, Drysdale, Gooch, Dinwiddie, Fauquier, Norborne Berkeley Lord de Botetourt, and Dunmore.

Here, as Vestrymen, worshipped the Hon. Daniel Parke; the Hon. John Page, "the immigrant;" Thomas Ludwell, Secretary of State; Sir John Randolph; Peyton Randolph, the King's Attorney and Speaker of the House of Burgesses; Robert Carter Nicholas, Treasurer of Virginia; Major Robert Beverly, Attorney, and Clerk of the House of Burgesses, and many others whose names appear in the long list of Vestrymen and upon the pages of the nation's history.

Here once sat the men who first saw the vision of a great free republic of this Western World, and who, at the altar of sacrifice, consecrated their lives to the cause of liberty which they loved—George Wythe, patriot, teacher, signer of the Declaration of Independence, was a vestryman; Thomas Jefferson, James Monroe, John Tyler, and Chief Justice John Marshall, and Edmund Randolph, worshipped here while students in the College of William and Mary; and most of them in after years while serving the Colony and State. George Mason, Edmund Pendleton, Edmund Randolph, Benjamin Harrison, Bland and Lee, while members of the House of Burgesses; Patrick Henry while a member of the House and Governor of Virginia (1776), and George Washington, while seeking to win the heart and hand of the beautiful Martha Custis.

These, and many others, whose names are deathless, have passed within these sacred courts and meekly bowed the knee in supplication to the King of Kings. As we linger in the silence of the Church, they pass before the awakened vision of the mind. They sit, as they did of old, listening to the law of the God of Nations, and to the message of liberty in the great Gospel of redemption. The walls of the cruciform old building seem to echo again with their voice of prayer and thanksgiving.

Here the youth of the nation that was to be, dreamed dreams and saw visions which awakened the high and noble aspirations of their lives; for here they heard the Gospel of Liberty, and engaged in the service of devotion and adoration which rouses the best that is in a man, and inspires him to live and serve for the Glory of his God and the good of his fellowman.

Here have ministered faithful servants of the most high God. The services have been almost continuous. The College Faculty could always be relied upon to supply ministerial service, and the City of Williamsburg, being the seat of the Colonial Government, created a constant demand for the services and ministrations of the Church.

The Church was preserved because it was needed. Thus the present building has been longer in continuous use than any other Episcopal Church in America.

Around the Church, side by side with the peers, warriors, scholars, and statesmen of the past in their sculptured tombs, beneath many mouldering heaps, "the rude forefathers of the hamlet sleep." Some to earthly fame are now unknown, the names of others live, not because they are engraved in marble, but because they helped to make the nation's history great.

The Old Church, with its historic associations and hallowed memories, is to us an inheritance from the past and a trust for the future. It must be preserved. It must remain to tell its story of the days that are gone to days that may yet be. It belongs, in a sense, to the nation with whose early history it is so intimately associated. It is doubly dear to us to whom it witnesses of the influence of our Church over the lives of the Nation-builders, and to whom it speaks of the continuity of our Church's life and liturgy.

The work of restoration, which has been determined upon, will be done with reverence and with devotion. The exterior will be left unchanged, for change here would mean innovation. The interior, which was changed and distorted, in view of conditions which no longer exists, will be restored to its ancient form, and the whole will be transmitted, under the good providence of God, to posterity as it was planned and builded and used by our forefathers.

✖ Historical Notes ✖

Original Parishes

IN 1632 Middle Plantation (subsequently Williamsburg) was "laid out and paled in."[1] A Parish bearing this name was created shortly thereafter[2] In 1644 a parish in James City was created called "Harrop Parish," which on April 1st, 1648, was united with Middle Plantation, forming Middletown Parish.

In 1674 the parish of Marston (established in York county in 1654) and Middletown Parish were united and became known as BRUTON PARISH.

Of the early history of Middle Plantation, or Williamsburg, little is known. The early court records have been destroyed, and there was no vestry-book preserved prior to the one of 1674. There was, however, a Church at Williamsburg in 1665. This fact is established by an entry in the vestry-book of Middlesex Parish, made in 1665, which directs that a Church be built in that parish after the

---

[1] Hening I, 139, 199, 208.
[2] York Records.

model of the one in Williamsburg.[1] This was doubtless a wooden structure. How long it had then been in use is not known.

The Name of the Parish

The name BRUTON was doubtless given to the Parish in honor of Thomas Ludwell, Esq., who, according to the record inscribed on his tombstone at the door of Bruton Church, was born in Bruton, in the County of Summerset, England, and departed this life in the year 1678.[2]

Old Vestry Records Relating to Church Building, Etc.

The first entry in the Vestry-book bears date "April Ye 18th, 1674," and on that day we find present at the Vestry meeting:

"The Honourable Coll: Danl. Parke, Mr. Rowland Jones, Minister, Mr. John Page, Mr. James Besouth, Mr. Robt. Cobb and Mr. Bray.,—Capt. Chesley, and Mr. Aylett, Church Wardens. Mr. John Owens, Sidesman. There being in the last levie Eight Thousand five hundred pounds of tobacco in Caske, Levyed to the Honourable Thomas Ludwell, Secretary, and Daniel Parke, Esq., 25 pound sterling, due to them upon ye purchase of ye Gleabe," &c.

In Nov. 1677, the vestry concluded that: "Whereas, upon ye Visiting of the Parishes, It was fully agreed that neither the Upper Church, nor the lower Church should be repaired, but a New Church should be built with brick, att the Middle Plantation,—Now in respect of the late troubles and Leavies this Yeare, It is by this Vestry Ordered that the next laying of the Leavie for this parish, the Demen-

---

[1] Bishop Meade's *Old Churches and Families in Virginia*.

[2] Sir William Berkeley, Governor, whose widow, Lady Frances Berkeley, Col. Phierp Ludwell married, was also from Bruton, England.

sions and order of building a New Church, and by whom to be Undertaken, be there fully determined; and that the present Church Wardens be desired to take Subscriptions from ye Honorable Thomas Ludwell, Daniel Parke, Esq., Major Jo: Page, of their former promises: and also of all other Gentlemen who will freely subscribe their benevolence to so Christian a work."

"There were then, probably, three wooden structures for worship in the Parish, corresponding to Middle Plantation, Harrop, and Marston parishes, all three of which now composed Bruton, which stretched in an irregular manner from York River to James River, and was about ten miles square. We have evidence certainly of the existence of two such churches: Marston Church is constantly referred to in the York county records as being in the direction of the present Biglow's "in the Indian fields near Queen's Creek;" and in December, 1674, Thomas Claiborne and Sarah, his wife (who was Sarah Fenn), joined in a deed to convey the wife's inheritance in the old plantation of Ralph Simkins at Middle Plantation, "except the two acres on wch the Parish Church of Bruton *now standeth*, formerly given by Ralph Simkins unto the parishioners of Bruton."

On Nov. 14th, 1678

"It is ordered that ye Subscriptions of free donations for building a brick Church be entered in the Register, and that Copies be given to the Church Wardens to procure all other persons' free donations that are dwellers in ye parish and when they have promised what they can, that a Vestrie be called for further consideration concerning the said Church."

Under the same date appears the following:

"I, John Page, doe oblige Myself, My heires, Executors, to pay or cause to be paid, Twenty pounds sterling to the Vestry of Bruton Parish, ffor and towards Build-

---

[1] Pres't Lyon G. Tyler.

ing of a Brick Church att Middle Plantation, for ye sd parish, upon demand. Witness my hand this 14th of November, 1678.

    Also I do promise to give land sufficient for the Church and Church Yard.   John Page

Witness
  Abraham Vinckler,
  Richard Curteen.

    I, Rowland Jones, Clerke, do oblige Myself, My heires, Executors, to pay or cause to be paid, five pounds sterling, to the Vestry of Bruton Parish, for and towards the building a brick Church, at the Middle Plantation, for ye said Parish, upon demand, as witness My hand, November ye 14, 1678.

Witness
  Richard Curteen,
  Abraham Vinckler.

    Wee, the subscribers, do hereby oblige ourselves, our heires, and Executors, and Administrators, to pay each of us five pounds Sterling to the Vestry, upon demand, towards ye building of A Brick Church, on ye Middle Plantation, for ye said Parish, as witness our hands this 14th of November, 1678.

Witness
  Abraham Vinckler,
  Richard Curteen.

          James Besouth,   Martin Gardner,
          Wm. Aylett,   Gideon Macon,
          Robert Cobb,   Tho. Taylor,
          Robert Spring,   Christo Pearson."

    On the 5th June, 1679, a full description of the Church to be built is given, together with articles of agreement between the Vestry and George Marable, the contractor of the work, which was to cost £350 sterling.

A COLONIAL SCENE.
From a painting of Bruton Church, now in the Metropolitan Museum of Art.

Owing to some disagreement we find the following entry:

"Whereas Mr. Geo. Marable hath arrested Mr. George Poyndexter and Mr. George Martin, (members of this Vestry,) in an action of the case to ye 4th day of ye next Generall Court: this Vestry do ordain and appoint Major Robert Beverly their lawfull Attorney on the behalf of ye said Parish, to answer ye suit of ye said George Marable, and also to procure judgment for performance of ye arts of agreement made by ye said Mr. George Marable," etc.

On the same occasion there is the record of a statement from Philip Ludwell, Esq., of a legacy by his brother Thomas Ludwell of £20 sterling and a promise for himself of £10 sterling towards the New Church to be built at Middle Plantation.[1]

On the 23d June, 1681, an agreement was made between the Vestry and Capt. Francis Page to build the Church at the same place, but with several variations from Marable's plan, for £150 sterling; "and sixty pounds of good, sound, merchantable sweet scented Tobacco and Caske, to be levied of each Tytheable in the parish for three years together—the first payment to commence this next ensuing crop."

Church Completed and Dedicated

"November ye 29th 1683."

The Parish Church is at length completed, and the Vestry notice the fact by the following: "Whereas ye Brick Church at Middle Plantation is now finished, It is ordered yt all ye Inhabitants of ye said Parish, do for the future repair thither to hear Divine Service, and ye Word of God preached; And that Mr. Rowland Jones, Minister, do dedicate ye said Church ye Sixth of January next, being ye Epiphany. And that Alexander Bonyman, Clerke, sett up

---
[1] McCabe.

notice at ye Mill, to give notice thereof; And that ye Ornaments, etc., be removed pr ye Church Wardens, and also yt ye old Communion Table be removed to ye minister's house and there remain."

Dr. McCabe remarks that this service of dedication was doubtless celebrated by more than the demonstrations contemplated by canons and rubrics, for immediately following this order is another that: "Mr. Roger Jones having promised to furnish ye Parish with two barrels of Tar, Each containing twenty-eight gallons, to be delivered at Middle Plantation, which being performed ye Parish is to pay ye said Mr. Jones after ye rate of £12 pr barrell."

It is to be remembered that these old Colonial Churches were never consecrated according to rubrical direction, as there was in those days no resident and no visiting Bishop to perform the service as ordered in the Book of Common Prayer.

On Oct. 31, 1684, a Committee is appointed to examine the work done on the New Church, and report Nov. 10th. Capt. Francis Page thereupon gives bond and security to keep the Church in good order and repair for four years.[1]

On May 10, 1686, there appears the following: "Whereas there is a proposition to the Vestry, concerning a Steeple and a Ring of Bells, the Vestry do request Mr. Rowland Jones, Mr. Martin Gardner, and Ffra Page, that they make a computation of the charge of building the Steeple and cost of the bells, and returne the same to ye next Vestry; and that in ye mean time they endeavour to procure what donations they can from such persons as may be thereto willing."

Fees of Clerk and Sexton

The fees of the Clerk at this time were ordered to be "three pounds of Tobacco for registering every Christening

---
[1] McCabe.

Historical Notes 17

and burial in ye Parish, and ye Sexton to have ten of Tobacco for every grave that he diggs."

"The last meeting of the Vestry, which the Revd. Rowland Jones attended, was held on the 26th day of November, 1687. This gentleman attended for the first time a meeting of the Vestry May 4th, 1675. On that day, "by a General Consent," they "subscribed a request to the Right Honorable Governour for an Induction into this Parish of Mr. Rowland Jones, minister." There is no evidence on the record that he ever was inducted, and yet he served them for twelve years, and then "fell asleep,"—for at the next Vestry Meeting, "June ye 5th, 1688," it was entered on the book as follows :[1]

"Whereas this Parish, by ye death of ye Rev. Mr. Rowland Jones, is destitute of a Minister, and Mr. James Sclater having offered to serve ye Parish in that quality, It is therefore agreed upon and ordered, that Mr. James Sclater be paid after ye rate of 6,000 pounds of tobacco per annum for six months. Ye time to commence from ye 13th day of May, 1688, and for such further time as he shall officiate in this Parish, to be allowed after the same rate proportionable. The said Mr. Sclater agreeing to preach a Sermon every other Sunday in the afternoon, if weather permit, and hath promised to administer ye Sacrament twice in ye six months; and each Sunday that he preach here to perform other rites and ceremonies of the Church."

Dr. McCabe, upon the authority of the Vestry book, states that this arrangement continued for a *very* short period, and that on the following July the same order was made in favor of Rev. Mr. Samuel Eburne, and the same requirements expressed. On November 9, 1688, the order was reiterated to continue in force until next Christmas. After this time it was determined that if Mr. Eburne agreed to officiate for seven years, he was to receive

---

[1] McCabe.

annually 16,666 pounds of tobacco and caske, with the use of the Glebe, and all the houses thereon.

On November 28, 1688, the following letter from Lord Howard Effingham, Governor of the colony, was received and recorded on the Vestry book:

"Gentlemen,—I understand that upon my former recommendation to you of Mr. Samuel Eburne, you have received him, and he hath continued to exercise his functions in preaching to you and performing Divine Service. I have now to recommend him ye second time to you, with ye addition of my own experience of his ability and true qualification in all points; together with his exemplary life and conversation. And, therefore, holding of him in the esteem of a person who, to God's honor and your good instruction, is fitt to be received, I do desire he may be by you entertained and continued; and that you will give him such encouragement as you have formerly done to persons so qualified.

"Effingham.

"8br 25, 1688."

A Silver Server Given

"The seaventh day of April, 1694.

His Excellency Sir Edmund Andros, Knight, was pleased to give to Bruton Parish A Large Silver Server."

"At a Vestry held for Bruton Parish ye 10th day of May, 1694,

Mr. Samuel Eburne, Minister, Mr. Hugh Norwell,
Edmd. Jennings, Esq. Mr. Henry Tyler,
Mr. Phil. Ludwell, Mr. John Kendall,
Mr. Daniel Darke, Mr. Ro. Crawley,
Mr. John Dorman, Mr. Baldwin Matthews,
Mr. Wm. Pinkethman,

His excellency having been pleased to bestow on ye Church a large silver server,—The Vestry therefore do desire Mr. Eburne, with Mr. Phil. Ludwell and Mr. Baldwin Matthews, ye Churchwardens, to wait upon his Excellency to render him thanks for his noble and pious gift."

The Church had begun to show signs of decay, and on May 6, 1693, there is the following: "Whereas ye inside work on ye Church ought to be rectified and repaired, it is therefore ordered that the.... Churchwardens provide an able workman to effect the same, and that it be done as soon as they can."

In 1694 the following is recorded in the Vestry-book: "Whereas severall Quakers there are in this Parish that are in arrears for their Parish dues,—It is therefore ordered that ye Church Wardens do demand and receive ye same this present year." And on the first November, same year, "Upon Mr. Eburne's proposition to ye Vestry, to be resolved whether they would sustain him for a longer time after his present time by agreement is expired, It is the opinion of this Vestry, and accordingly ordered that it shall be referred to the Vestry that shall meet for this Parish upon Easter Tuesday next." And on "Ye third day of Aprill, 1695, in answer to Mr. Eburne's proposition, this Vestry ordered that no Minister be hereafter entertained but from year to year, and that they allow and pay him only according to law. Upon which Mr. Eburne doth refuse to stay any longer than till next Christmas." On the 15th January, 1696, "It is ordered that Mr. Saml. Eburne, Minister, be allowed two hundred pounds of tobacco and caske, it being for preaching four Sermons after the time by agreement having expired." "The said Mr. Saml. Eburne declaring his Intentions of leaving this Country, ye Church Wardens, therefore, are requested (as often as they can) to procure a Minister. And when there shall be no Minister, the Clerke is ordered to Read Homilies and prayers. And likewise ye said Church Wardens are requested to wait upon his Excellency ye Governor, and pray him that he would be pleased to have this Parish in his thoughts when any Ministers shall arrive here out of England."

Mr. Eburne was not permitted to leave without a

resolution expressing the esteem and high regard of the Vestry for him as a man and as a Minister. He had served among them for seven years, and had, in those days when Ministers were not always what they should have been, won for himself a good testimonial which is cordially expressed by the Vestry in the following resolution:

"We, the Vestry of Bruton Parish, in Virginia, whose names are underwritten, do certifie all whom it may concerne, that Mr. Samuel Eburne, Minister of the said Parish, hath so well behaved himself in all his Ministeriall ffunctions amongst us for the space of seven years and upwards, that we do all unanimously desire his further continuance with us; but, by reason of his growing into years, he hath chosen to go into a warmer climate.

<table>
<tr><td>Daniel Parke,</td><td>John Kendall,</td></tr>
<tr><td>Edmd. Jennings,</td><td>Hugh Norwell,</td></tr>
<tr><td>John Owens,</td><td>Philip Ludwell, Jr.</td></tr>
<tr><td>Robert Crawley,</td><td>John Dormar,</td></tr>
<tr><td>Henry Tyler,</td><td>Timo. Pinckethman."</td></tr>
<tr><td>Wm. Pinkethman,</td><td></td></tr>
</table>

In April, 1697, Mr. Cope Doyley's name appears as Minister, and "it is ordered that Mr. Doyley be entertained as Minister of this Parish, with ye yearly allowance according to law." On the 14th October, 1698, "Whereas there are severall Quakers in arrears for Parish Levies, it is ordered that the Church Wardens do prosecute them to ye County Court where the debt is actionable."

Jamestown Abandoned

In 1699, during the second term of the administration of Governor Francis Nicholson, the seat of government was moved from Jamestown to Williamsburg "on account of the prevalence of malaria and mosquitos" at Jamestown,[1] and because "the air was serene and temperate

---

[1] Rev. Hugh Jones—*Present State of Virginia.*

The Old Church Tower at Jamestown.

Historical Notes

and crystal springs burst from dry and champaign soil"[1] around Williamsburg.

Old Jamestown is now lonely and deserted. The tower of the Old Church stands,

> "Lone relic of the past! old mouldering pile,
> Where twines the ivy round its ruins gray."

The foundation walls of the Old Church have been unearthed and sheltered in by the "Association for the Preservation of Virginia Antiquities." The pilgrim standing amid the sacred ruins of these old Churches has suggested to him the beautiful lines inscribed by some unknown one upon the walls of Old Blandford Church, in Petersburg, Virginia:[2]

> "Thou art crumbling to the dust, old pile,
>   Thou art hastening to thy fall,
> And around thee in thy loneliness
>   Clings the ivy to thy wall.
> The worshippers are scatter'd now
>   Who met before thy shrine,
> And silence reigns where anthems rose
>   In days of auld lang syne.
>
> "And rudely sighs the wandering wind
>   Where oft, in years gone by,
> Prayer rose from many hearts to Him,
>   The highest of the high.
> The tramp of many a busy foot
>   Which sought thy aisles is o'er,
> And many a weary heart around
>   Is still'd for evermore.
>
> "How oft ambition's hope takes wing:
>   How droop the spirits now:
> *We hear the distant city's din:*
>   The dead are mute below.
> The sun which shone upon their paths
>   Now gilds their lonely graves;
> The zephyrs which once fann'd their brows
>   The grass above them waves.

---

[1] Hening.
[2] Old Blandford Church, built in 1737, is now being restored.

> "Oh, could we call the many back
> Who've gather'd here in vain,
> Who careless roved where we do now,
> Who'll never meet again,—
> How would our souls be stirr'd
> To meet the earnest gaze
> Of the lovely and the beautiful,
> The light of other days."

We hear now no "distant city's din." James City is no more. "The air a solemn stillness holds," broken only by the murmur of the waves, beating ceaselessly upon the shore, which is gradually receding at their touch.

When the Church at Jamestown was abandoned the Font and the Communion Service were brought to Bruton Church. (See illustrations.) Parish tradition claims this Font to be the one still in use in the Bruton Parish Church. The inscription on the Communion silver establishes its identity beyond question.

In 1699, the Church again stands in need of repairs, which are ordered. In 1700, Gov. Nicholson requires a certificate that Mr. Doyley reads prayers every Sunday at the Parish Church, which question is answered by the Vestry in the affirmative. This would indicate that the Governor had not yet removed his residence to Williamsburg, as he would otherwise have been acquainted with the regularity of Service in the Parish Church.

The last Vestry meeting attended by Mr. Doyley was Nov. 5, 1691. His death is announced Oct. 7, 1702. Mr. Solomon Wheatley is invited to preach for them preparatory to a "call," which takes place very soon thereafter, (Dec. 13, 1702;) and again in Dec. 1702, are repairs in brick and wood ordered upon the Church. In 1703 a new pulpit is required, the pews ordered to be repaired, the floor raised, &c. On the 11th of November, of that year, Mr. Whateley (spelt Wheatley in preceding records) desires to know whether he is to be retained, and on the 10th of the following February he is informed that his "time by agreement being expired last Christmas, the Vestry not thinking it proper to enter-

Historical Notes 23

tain him another year, to ye end that he should not be put to an inconvenience, have granted his staying to officiate in ye Parish till ye 25th of March next, to ye end he may provide himself elsewhere." "Coll. Ludwell is requested by ye Vestry to write to Mr. Isaac Grace, that arrived lately in ye ship Bartwell, to request him to give the Parish a Sermon as soon as conveniently," the result of which application to the Rev. Gentleman is given below:

"At a Vestry held ye 3d day of May, 1704, Coll. Ludwell acquainted this Vestry that pursuant to an order of Vestry, ye 10th day of ffebruary last, he had desired Mr. Isaac Grace to give ye Parish a Sermon, to ye end that if ye Vestry did like him, he might be entertained as Minister of this Parish. To which Mr. Grace answered that his Excellency had knowledge of the matter, and had forbid him to be concerned with ye Parish. And added that he should be glad of so good a Parish, if he might have it of ye Governour's likeing; but as the Governor had forbid him, he dare not meddle with it."

Conflict as to Right of Induction

The independent action of the Vestry in dismissing Rev. Solomon Whateley roused the Governor to opposition. A stubborn conflict ensued. The Vestry resolutely refused to have a Minister inducted into the Parish. They claimed the independent right to call whom they pleased, and to make terms suitable to themselves as to the length of service. The Governor claimed that under English law he had the right, as a representative of the Sovereign power of England, to induct the clergy. Both parties in the controversy seem to have been in a somewhat tempestuous frame of mind. Rev. Mr. Grace very strongly insinuated that the Vestry, or some one in it, had not told the truth. The records would indicate that he himself had a very treacherous memory or a very erring tongue. The correspondence in this case is given in Appendix A.

It resulted in the election of Mr. Whateley, the Governor's candidate, as Minister, but with the rights of the Vestry distinctly asserted in the call extended.

Vestrymen

Of these early Vestrymen Thomas Jefferson said: "The Vestrymen are usually the most discreet farmers, so distributed through the parish that every part of it may be under the immediate eye of some one of them. They are well acquainted with the details and economy of private life, and they find sufficient inducements to execute their charge well, in their philantrophy, in the approbation of their neighbors, and the distinction which it gives them."[1]

John Fisk quotes the above statement as showing the difference between the concentrated town government of New England, with the congregational Church as its formative center, and the county system of government in Virginia, with the Vestrymen of the parish representing the widely scattered population of the country in the management of ecclesiastical affairs. Williamsburg, being the seat of the Colonial government, constituted a more concentrated population, and furnished the Church with a more representative body of Vestrymen. The country constituency was, however, constantly represented by gentlemen still living upon their ancestral estates.

The business of these Colonial Vestrymen was such as to train them for service in a representative government. They were elected to represent the congregation. It was their duty to see that judicious measures were enacted by the House of Burgesses for the support of the Church, and for safe-guarding religion, and when these laws were passed it became their duty to see that they were enforced. The parish poor were committed to their oversight and care. They were empowered to make levies for this pur-

---

[1] Quoted by John Fisk in *Civil Government in the United States*, p. 60.

pose. It was their duty to apportion levies for the maintenance of the Church, and they were given authority, under law, to collect these taxes, if necessary, by civil process. They thus acted as representatives of the people in the conduct of this large and important part of their affairs. The position was one of responsibility and honor. The Vestry Meetings were of vital importance to the community, and were not anticipated with any degree of pleasure by those who had absented themselves from service without excuse, or who had gone there and behaved in an unseemly way. Bishop Meade has shown that the men who served the colony and commonwealth in these early days were almost without exception men who had gained experience as representatives of the people through service as parish vestrymen. They were the men to whom the Church, and the state, naturally looked for leadership, and neither looked to them in vain.

"At a Vestry held for Bruton Parish, ye 7th July, 1705, Mr. Henry Tyler is desired to procure Carpenters to Visit the Church, and to report their opinion to ye next Vestry whether it can be repaired or not. If it Can be repaired, what stuff will be necessary for the same, and what they will undertake to do it for."

From the following entry it would seem that Governor Nicholson desired to conciliate the Vestry after the arrogant display of his authority as manifested in the induction controversy, but it would also appear that the Vestry still maintained their spirit of courage and independence:

"At a Vestry held for Bruton Parish ye 7th August, 1705," .... "His Excellency the Governour sending to this Vestry (by ye hand of Mr. Wm. Robertson) An Altar Cloth and Cushion as a present for ye use of ye Parish, together with fifty shillings for ye use of ye poor, and desiring ye said gift of fifty shillings might be recorded in the Vestry book as being his Excellency's usual quarterly gift; and also what his

Excellency hath formerly given, together with an account how ye same hath been disposed of,—The Vestry return this answer by Mr. Robertson, (viz.) We return his Excellency many thanks for ye Altar Cloth, and also for ye fifty shillings now sent—which we assure his Excellency's shall be registered; but not knowing it to be his Excellency's Constant Custom, we cannot register it as such without we know att present what his Excellency hath given to the poor; but we do promise to examine that matter against ye next Vestry, and what appears to us, then shall be registered."

As to the thoroughness of this investigation, and its result, we are not told. His Excellency gets no further credit for his accustomed benevolence. He sends no more *quarterly* offerings.

On November 20th, 1710, the decease of Rev. Solomon Whateley is thus announced: "Having had the Misfortune at this present to be without a Minister, By ye death of ye Revd. Solomon Whateley,—It is ordered that the Church Wardens (for supplying the Parish with Ministers to preach weekly, while the Parish continues vacant) do desire the severall Ministers hereafter named, to preach in this Parish Church on the severall Sunday Mornings they shall appoint,— for which services they shall be paid four hundred pounds of Tobacco in this Parish for each Sermon. The Church Wardens are ordered to wait on ye honorable the Governor,[1] with ye proceedings of ye Vestry herein.

"The Ministers desired to preach weekly are, upon 3d of December, the Revd. Mr. Tillyard:

December 10, the Revd. Mr. Slaughter, (Sclater,)
" 17, " " Mr. Paxton,
" 14, " " Mr. Commissary, (Blair;)
" 31, " " Mr. Goodwin;
January 7, " " Mr. Wallace;
" 14, " " Mr. Taylor."

---

[1] Edmund Jennings, who succeeded Gov. Nott, who died in 1706, and is buried in Bruton Church Yard.

Historical Notes

On Dec. 10th, 1710, "Ordered—That whereas there was an Order made the last Vestry for 7 Ministers to preach on certain Sundays, wherein the Revd. James Sclater was one;— It is ordered by this Meeting that the said Sclater be left out of the number, and that the Church Wardens give notice to the Rev. Arthur Tillyard to preach December 10th, and the rest in their order."

Commissary Blair, Minister

From portrait in the library of William and Mary College.

The Bishop of London, who had jurisdiction over the Colony of Virginia, induced Rev. Dr. James Blair to come to Virginia as a missionary in 1685. In 1689 he was appointed Commissary of the Bishop, and commissioned, as his representative, to make visitations in territory assigned, deliver charges, inspect the churches, and, when necessary, administer discipline. Not being a Bishop, he, of course, could not Confirm, or administer Ordination, or consecrate churches. He held this office, and discharged its functions, together with his other ministerial and educational duties, for fifty-three years. On December 10th, 1710, he was elected Minister of Bruton Church, which position he held until his death in 1742. The Vestry Book contained the following records relating to his election and ministry: December 10th, 1710, "Upon the reading of the Revd. Benjamin Goodwin and the Revd. James Blair's letters, wherein they set forth their desire to be admitted Ministers of Bruton Parish, now vacant by the Death of the Revd. Solomon Whateley;—The Matter being debated, the Question was putt whether it should be decided by Vote.

"Resolved in the affirmative—present the Honble. Edwd. Jennings. Whereupon the Meeting proceeded to the choice of a Minister for Bruton Parish, and by the Majority of Votes the Revd. James Blair was elected Minister thereof.

"Ordered, The Church Wardens acquaint ye Reverend James Blair, that upon reading his letter, wherein was Sett forth his desire to be their Minister, The Vestry proceeded to the consideration thereof, and accordingly made choice of him to be their Minister for the next ensuing year.—Ordered, that the Church Wardens appoint a Vestry as soon as possible to entertain him accordingly."

Dr. Blair's letter to the Vestry is as follows:

December 4th, 1710.

"Gentlemen:

"The great importance of yt deliberation ye are now upon, how to supply this Parish with a Minister who shall discharge his duty in so Eminent a Station as becomes him both for Life and Doctrine, together with the happiness I enjoy in your Neyborhood and acquaintance; and the great conveniency of my habitation in the heart of your Parish, with several assurances from persons of eminent note that such a proffer may be acceptable, Induce me to take this Opportunity of acquainting You that if My Service may be approved in that Station, ye shall need to look noe farther for a Minister.

"It is true, I have soe many obligations to ye Parish of James City, that nothing but the urgent Necessity of health, often impaired by such long Winter Journeys, and a fear that as age and Infirmities increase, I shall not be able to attend that Service (being at such a distance) so punctually as I have hitherto done, could have induced me to entertain anything as of leaving them. If ye Shall think fitt to approve of this My proposal, I hope ye shall have noe occasion to repent your choice, and that I may have further opportunities by my diligence in My Ministeriall functions among you to shew how ready I am to approve Myself.

Gentlemen, Your most faithfull humble servt. to my parishioners,

James Blair.

Vera Copia Teste
C. Jackson, Clerk Vestry."

On the 28th of December, 1710, "Mr. Hugh Norwell reported, that pursuant to an order made under last Vestry, he had acquainted the Revd. James Blair, that the Gentlemen of the Vestry had considered his Letter, and, according to the Desire thereof, had made choice of him to be their Minister, and that this Vestry was called to treat with him.

"The Revd. James Blair being present, it was mutually agreed that the said James Blair be entertained as Minister of Bruton Parish, for the Year next ensuing the date."

The following notes, relative to the ministry and work of Commissary Blair, were recorded in the old Vestry book under the dates indicated:

On the 6th July, 1721, Mr. Commissary Blair notifies the Vestry that "he is obliged to repair for England upon an urgent occasion; and that he intends to return hither again as soon as his affairs will permit, and proposing that during his absence the best care shall be taken for a supply of Ministers to execute office in this Parish, and also agreeing to demand no salary in that time; and thereupon desiring that the Vestry will not make application for any other Incumbent to the cure of this Parish, for the space of twelve months," &c. &c.

On the 23d Nov., 1722, "The Rev. Mr. Commissary Blair" is again at his post at the Vestry Meeting.

On the 12th December, 1725, "Lewis Burwell, Gent., being elected Vestryman for this Parish, this day took the Oath appointed by act of Parliament to be taken instead of the Oaths of Allegiance and Supremacy, the Abjuration Oath, Subscribed the test, and also subscribed to be Conformable to the Doctrine and Discipline of the Church of England."

"At a Vestry held for Bruton Parish, the 22 day of June, 1726, The Revd. James Blair, Minister of this Parish, acquainting the Vestry that at the request of the Governors of this College he has undertaken a Voyage for England, in Order to Obtain a Transfer, and to Negotiate other important Affairs of the College; to the end the good and pious design of that building, so usefull and beneficial to this Country, may be speedily accomplished, and presenting the Vestry a list of Ministers which he proposes shall officiate in his absence,—The same was accordingly agreed to and accepted. The said Mr. Blair laying before the Vestry an account of the poor's Money, whereby it appears that the Sum of £26 11s. 1d. is due to the poor's bag;—Ordered that the same be paid into the hands of Mr. John Blair, to be disposed of as the Church Wardens and Vestrymen shall appoint."

On the 16th day of November, 1727, Mr. Commissary Blair is in his place again in Vestry meeting.

The Jamestown Baptismal Font.

The Silver-Gold Communion Service,
known as the "Queen Anne Set."

The Church of 1715

ETURNING to the historical continuity of the old Vestry book, we find the following notes relative to the Church of 1715, which was built during the ministry of Revd. Mr. Blair, upon the foundation of the Church of 1683. This is the building still in use.

"Att a Vestry held the ffirst day of October, 1706, The Vestry considering ye great charge ye parish hath been at for ye repairing of ye Church, and how bad a condition it is still in,—Ordered, that twenty thousand pounds of Tobacco be levied this year for and towards building of a new Church."

"November ye 14, 1706. Whereas there is levyed thirty-one pound of Tobacco per pole for and towards ye building A New Church, Any of ye parishioners have hereby ye liberty to pay ye same in money after ye rate of ten shillings pr cwt: when other parish dues are collected."

"Att a Vestry held for Bruton Parish, December 10, 1710, Present, Hon Edmd. Jennings, Esq."
(Here follow the names of the Vestry.)

"Upon the representation of the Hon. Edmd. Jennings that Mr. John Holloway and himself had discoursed upon the business concerning the appropriating a sum of money towards the building a Church in Bruton Parish, and that Mr. John Holloway was pleased to say He did believe he could prevail with the House (of Burgesses) to appropriate £200 for that use, and that the House was desirous the gentlemen of the Vestry should give them a meeting on this day, which was the occasion of calling this Vestry to consider what might be necessary concerning the same,—

"Ordered, That the Church Wardens goe and acquaint the House of Burgesses, that the Gentlemen of the Vestry were ready to wait upon them when they should appoint."

"Having Delivered their Message, they returned and acquainted this Meeting that the House had appointed Mr. John Holloway, Mr. Nicholas Merriwether, and Mr. Robert Bolling, to wait upon the Vestry and hear their proposals."

"Then this Meeting proceeded to consider what sume of Money and what Dimentions might be necessary for the building a Church to serve their own paritioners, Provided the House of Burgesses would not contribute towards the Building thereof. The matter being debated it was Resolved, that a Church of ye same dimentions of ye old church will be large enough, and that £500 would be sufficient for the building thereof."

"Mr. Jno. Holloway, Mr. Robert Bolling and Mr. Nicholas Merriwether, delivered a Message (from the House of Burgesses) to this effect, that the House was willing to appropriate a Sufficient sume of Money for the building pews for the Governr., Council and House of Burgesses; They further added they were to enquire what Dimentions were necessary for a Church for the Parish, and what sume of money would be sufficient for the Building the same;— Whereupon the Honble. Edwd. Jennings informed them the Gentlemen of the Vestry were of opinion a Church of the same Dimentions of the Old Church would be large enough, and that £500 would be sufficient for the building the same."

"The Gentlemen of the Vestry further added, They did not in the least doubt but the House of Burgesses would shew their Pious and Generous spirits by their Liberall Donations towards Soe necessary and good a worke; and that they could assure them to the best of their Judgments they would appropriate the same according to the true Intent thereof."

At the same meeting it was "Ordered, That whoever shall be admitted to serve as Minister in this Parish, shall have no Induction."

Historical Notes   33

Plan Submitted by Honble. Alexr. Spottswood.

"At a Meeting of the Vestry, held for ye Parish of Bruton, March 1st, 1711, Present, James Blair, Clerk,
(Here follow the names of the Vestrymen.)

"Upon ye Information of James Blair, Clerk, that he had received from the Honble. Alexr. Spottswood, a platt or draught of a Church, (whose length 75 foot, and bredth 28 foot in the clear, with two wings on each side, whose width is 22 foot,) which he Laid before the Vestry for approbation—Adding further, that ye Honble. ye Governor proposed to the Vestry to build only 53 of the 75 foot, and that he would take care for the remaining part.

"The Vestry proceeded to the immediate consideration of the commodiousness and conveniency of the said Platt or Draught: which is approved of.

"It being moved that the charge of such part be computed, the Vestry not knowing what scantlings were suitable for such a building, nor the number of bricks the said worke would take—is referred.

"Ordered, That Christo. Jackson, Clarke, be impowered to agree with some skillful workman, to lay down the said scantlings: also to calculate the number of bricks sufficient for a wall of 56 foot long, 28 foot wide, and 23 foot high above ground, and report the same to the next Vestry, in order to a full consideration thereof.

"Ordered, therefore, that Capt. Frederick Jones acquaint the Honble. Alexr. Spottswood with the proceedings of the Vestry concerning his draught.

"The Revd. James Blair moving that new prayer-books for the Minister and Clerke be sent for,—Ordered, that new ones be sent for, and that ye Church Wardens request the assistance of ye Honble. Edmd. Jennings in buying ye same."

On the 15th March, 1711, the proposals of Mr. John Tillet and Mr. Henry Cary, were submitted to the Vestry, for furnishing the materials with which to build the Church, but both being considered entirely too exorbitant, "Whereupon ye Honorable Alex'r Spottswood proposed together with ye Hon. Edmund Jennings, to deliver in place as many bricks as shall be thought necessary in building ye Church, at ye rate of 15s. per thousand, in order to beat down ye extravagant prices of workmen, provided some of ye Vestry would undertake other parts." On the 17th Nov. 1711, the contractor for the building the Church, all preliminaries being settled, is allowed till "the 15 October, 1714, for building the same." The contractor was James Morris, and the deeds were at the same Vestry, ordered to be drawn up by Stephen Thompson.

On the 28th March, 1712, a new draught of the Church is ordered.

In the Calendar of State Papers, Volume 1, Page 174, under date December, 1713. "The Dimensions of ye two Wings of Bruton Parish Church, together with ye Rates of ye Materials and Workmanship therein required is given," which has been copied to show the Dimensions and the cost of Materials and Workmanship at this date.

DIMENSIONS

The inside Breadth of each Wing, or the distance
 from ye East wall to ye West wall, must be....22 Foot
The inside Length of each Wing, or ye Distance
 from ye North wall to ye Body of ye Church
 must be..19 F——
The Breadth of ye East & West Windows............ 6 F——
The Breadth of ye North & South Windows......... 7 F——
The Breadth of ye North & South Doors............... 5 F——
The Thickness of ye Walls below ye Water Table 3 Bricks,
 & above ye same 2 Bricks length.
The Height of ye Walls & of ye Ceiling to be ye same with
 those of ye Body of ye Church.
The Rooff to rise in proportion to ye Breadth that it
 spans.

MATERIALS

The Bricks are to be rated at Seventeen Shills pr: Thousand.

The Lime at Six pence pr: Bushel.

The Sand at Eighteen pence pr: Load.

The Scantlines at £4 10 p: Thousand.

The Shingles at $12^s\ 6^d$ pr: Thous.

The whole Scaffolding Stuff, Chords & Plank at 3 Pounds.

WORKMANSHIP

The Laying of ye Bricks, including ye Labourers work, shall be rated at $7^s\ 6^d$ pr: Thousand.

The framing, raising and covering ye Roof at $18^{sh}\ 6^d$ p: Square.

The framing and Raising ye Floor at 10^{sh} pr: Square.

The Working and Setting ye Eves at 20^{sh} pr: foot.

The Rubbing, Cutting, & Setting ye Window Arches at 5^{sh} pr: Arch.

The Rubbing and Cutting ye Foot lesses at one penny pr: foot.

The Rubbing ye Returns at 2^{sh} pr: hundred.

The framing & Setting ye Window & Door Cases at 10^{sh} each.

On the 11th December, 1712, a sum of money, £10 sterling, in the hands of Mr. Richard Kendall, being a legacy from Mrs. Catharine Besouth, is ordered to be paid over to the Revd. James Blair, for a "Suitable piece of plate of ye same value, for the use of Bruton Parish, with this inscription upon it—(Ye Gift of Mrs. Catharine Besouth.")

December 2d, 1715. At length the new Church is finished, or nearly so.

Following this there are brief notes of interest. Nov. 16th, 1716. "Ordered that the Church Wardens dispose of all the materials belonging to the Old Church, except the bricks." The new Church is shingled in 1717.

December, 17, 1720. Mr. John Holloway is "recommended to send for a Church Bible and two Common Prayer Books, for the use of the Church."

In 1724 Rev. James Blair, reported to the Bishop of London, that the Church was provided with "A great Bible, 2 common prayer books, the Homilies, canons, pulpit Cloths, altar and altar piece, Font, Cushions, surplice, bell, etc.," and that "There were one hundred and ten families, and fifty communicants in the Parish." He also stated that at that time there were three hundred acres of Glebe land belonging to the Parish, and that the Parish was about ten miles square.[1]

On the 15th day of June, 1728, order is given for tearing down the ceiling of the Church and putting up a new one.

"At a Vestry held for Bruton Parish the 12 day of November, 1729, John Randolph, Esq., (knighted shortly after,) having been elected a Vestryman, this day took and Subscribed the Oaths appointed by Law to His Majesty's person and Government, &c."[2]

Nov. 6, 1740, the Vestry ordered Church and Churchyard to be repaired. Nov. 14, 1742, "The Church Bible given to the Parish by Capt. Matthews, being in danger of spoiling by lying in the chest, Mr. Thomas Cobbs agrees to take it, and to send for another when the same shall be required."

On the 3d Day of Decem., 1742, "The Vestry Resolved on the following articles" in relation to the repairs of the Church:

"The brick Ornaments of the Gavel ends to be taken down, and finished with wood, answering the rest. The whole roof to be Covered. The whole to be new pewed, and the pulpit placed in the South East Corner. The Church Yard to be repaired for the present in the Cheapest Manner."

---

[1] Perry, page 300.
[2] In June, 1903, a beautiful marble tablet was unveiled in the Chapel of the College of William and Mary to replace a similar tablet which had been erected to the memory of Sir John Randolph, which was destroyed when the College was burned.

Death of Commissary Blair and Election of Revd. Thos. Dawson

"At a Vestry held" the 6th day of May, 1743, the sad news is officially announced, that the Rev. Mr. Commissary Blair is no more. And there was entered the following note: And "Whereas by the Decease of the Revd. Mr. Commissary Blair," (who had served the Church of Bruton Parish for the space of thirty-two Years as its Minister; William and Mary College as its President for nearly fifty years, and as Commissary for fifty-three years,) late Minister of this Parish, the Cure is now Vacant. And Whereas the Rev. Mr. Thomas Dawson has for some time officiated for Mr. Commissary, in which he hath acquitted himself to the Universal good liking of this Parish, and also producing a letter from the Honble. the Governor, strongly recommending him to the Choice of the Vestry, they do therefore unanimously elect the said Mr. Thomas Dawson Minister of this Parish."

On the 9th May, 1744, it is Ordered that a foundation of brickwork be laid round the Isle to receive the floor; and the Isle be new layd with the same stone, the Church to be New Whitewashed, and plaistering to be repaired where wanting. Ordered likewise, that the pews be painted three times in Oile, and the South Gallery to be extended as far as the Corner."

Church Enlarged and Organ Secured

"At a Vestry held for Bruton Parish, August 22, 1744, "Resolved, that a petition be drawn to be preferred to the next General Assembly to request them to contribute towards the repairs of the two wings of the Church, which were formerly built at the expense of the public. And that they will be pleased to take into their Consideration, whether an organ, to be bought by the Public and Appropriated for the use of the Church of the Parish where the Governor resides and the General Assembly and the Courts are held, May not be Ornamental and useful in the Divine Service; and that Mr. Dawson, Mr. Wray, Mr. (John) Blair, Mr. Harmer and Mr. Waller prepare the same." After eight years delay, (according to Hening,) John Blair, Philip Ludwell, Armisted Burwell, James Power, and Benjamin Powell were appointed by the Assembly a committee to provide material for enlarging the Church and for purchasing and setting up an organ in the loft to cost £200.

On the 15th day of March, 1750-1, "The Honble. John Blair, Coll: Lewis Burwell, and Mr. John Holt, or any two of them, are impowered to treat with workmen for an addition to the Church, and to lay their proposals before the Vestry in order for their agreement thereto."

Pursuant to these orders, and the action of the House of Burgesses, the Church doubtless assumed its present proportions of 100 feet long, 28 feet wide, the wings being reduced from 19 feet to 14½ feet in length.[1] If the Church was originally built according to the first draft of Alex. Spottswood, the length of the West body, or nave, was 39 feet, the width of the transepts was 22 feet, and the length of the chancel end was 14 feet, making the total length 75 feet. An addition of 25 feet to the East, or chancel end of the building, would have made it 39 feet, which is its present length, corresponding to the length of the nave, and making the entire length of the building 100 feet. This 25 feet was either added by the order of 1750 or by the altered draft of 1712. No addition has has been made to the West end of the Church. The mention of the galleries located there proves this.

On August 11, 1747, "Peyton Randolph, Esq., is chosen a Vestryman."

---
[1] Tyler.

Church Yard Wall Built

December 14, 1749, the Vestry agree with Mr. Emery Hughes to build a brick wall around the Churchyard for £290. July 7th, 1752, "Emery Hughes having failed to perform his agreement".... in building the brick wall around the Church, Samuel Spurr agrees to do the same for £320, and gives bond and security to finish the work by October, 1754.

June 18, 1754, Mr. Robt. Carter Nicholas is chosen a Vestryman.

The name of George Wythe, the distinguished jurist and statesman, (the early patron of Henry Clay,) appears for the first time on the record as Vestryman and Churchwarden, 20th November, 1760; and on the 9th day of February, 1761, "The Reverend Wm. Yates is Unanimously Chosen Minister of this Parish in the Room of the Revd. Commissary Thomas Dawson, Dec'd."

On the 29th day of November, 1763, Rev. Mr. Yates attended the last Vestry meeting, and on the 5th day of October, 1764, his decease is recorded in the accounts of the Parish, where there stands an amount to his credit of tobacco, 17,280 lbs. Nov. 7th, 1764, Rev. Mr. James Horrocks, Commissary, is chosen as the Minister of the Parish.

Belfry Built

On October 6, 1768, "The Revd. Mr. James Horrocks, Peyton Randolph, Esq., Thomas Everard, Esq., Robert Carter Nicholas, Esq., and the Church Wardens, Mr. John Pierce and Mr. Wm. Eaton, or any four of them, are appointed a Committee to receive proposals for building a belfry to the Church."

On the 14th September, 1769, the Vestry, consisting of the names of men whose memory the Church in Virginia, and the State at large will not forget,—such as John Blair, Benjamin Waller, Lewis Burwell, Wm. Graves, Robert Carter Nicholas, Thomas Everard, George Wythe, Fred. Bryan, and Coll. John Prentis, "agreed with Benjamin Powell to build a Steeple and repair the Church for £410.—£150 to be paid this present Year, £130 the Next Year, and £130 in the Year 1771. He is to have the Old Bell, and the Materials of the old Steeple.

This order relating to the building of a new Steeple does not fix the date of the Old Tower upon which the old Steeple referred to stood. The Church Tower is not structually the same as the Church, and has the appearance of being older.

THE CHURCH AS SEEN FROM THE CHURCH YARD.

Some Old Vestry Orders

SCATTERED through the old Vestry Book were a number of orders of special purport which were given under different dates, and with reference to the subject indicated by the headings under which they have been arranged here for convenient reference.

Minister's Salary

Ninth of June, 1682, "Ordered that Mr. Rowland Jones, Minister, for the future shall be paid annually ye Sum of Sixteen thousand six hundred and sixty-six pounds of Tobacco and Caske. Any former order of Vestry to the contrary notwithstanding." Here follow the names and the sentence, Tester, Alex. Bonnyman. "Veritas non est dubitanda."

Church Attendance

June 9th, 1682. "The Vestry of this Parish takeing into consideration that many and divers of the inhabitants have been negligent in comeing to Church, tending to ye dishonor of God and the contempt of Government, Therefore the said Vestry have now ordered, That such person or persons inhabiting in this Parish, as shall be negligent herein, shall be presented by ye Church Wardens to ye Court, and then be proceeded with according to Law, and that publication hereof be made pr ye Clerke at both Churches." These Churches were, no doubt, one in the upper, and one in the lower portions of the Parish.

Private Pews

June 9th, 1682, "thought fit and likewise ordered, that Coll: Jno. Page may (might) have the privilege to sett a pew for himself and his ffamily in the Chancell of the new Church at Middle Plantation"—although the Church was not yet built. The privilege of setting up a pew in the Chancel, was subsequently accorded to the Hon. Philip Ludwell.

At a Vestry on Nov. 2, 1704,

"An order of Council is given by Mr. William Robertson, Clerk of ye Council, wherein is proposed that ye South side of ye Chancel of ye Church, (including ye pew where his Excellency now sits,) be fitted up as a pew for ye Governour & Council for ye time being, to be done by ye direction of Mr. Auditor Byrd, which is agreed to by this Vestry."

Church Yard Land

On November 14th, 1678, the land on which the Church was built, together with "sixty feet of the same, every way for a Church-yard," was the gift, forever, of the "Honourable Coll: John Page." Every receipt given by Francis Page, for moneys received for the new Church, is thus signed: "I say, Received pr Me ffra: Page."

"An act providing for laying out Williamsburg provided also for condemning land for the church, and the map of the town in the college library shows that the churchyard was so enlarged as to take in two acres on Duke of Gloucester street. Around three-fourths of this the brick wall was built, and its front is, on measurement, 330 feet. The other portion unenclosed was sold not many years ago to private land owners."[1]

Order Regulating Burial in the Church and Chancel

At a Vestry held the 31st October, 1684, present: "The Minister, Mr. Rowland Jones, the Hon. Philip Ludwell, Esq., the Hon. Jno. Page, Esq., the Hon. James Bray, Esq., ye Hon. Thos. Ball and Capt. ffrancis Page," &c., it was resolved that "ffor the privilege of Burials either in ye Chancell, or in ye new Church, it is ordered by this Vestry, that for breaking up ye ground in ye Chancell, ye ffees payable to

---

[1] Tyler.

Historical Notes

ye Minister shall be one thousand pounds of Tobacco, or five pounds sterling; and in ye Church ye ffee payable to the Parish shall be five hundred pounds of Tobacco, or fifty shillings in money; and that ye Minister be at ye charge to relay ye Chancell, and ye Parish for the same."

Order as to where Certain People should Sit in Church

January 9, 1716, it is "Ordered that the Men sitt on the North side of the Church, and the Women on the left.

"Ordered that Mr. Commissary Blair sitt in the head pew in the Church, and that he may Carry any Minister into the same.

"Ordered that the Parishioners be seated in the Church, and none others.

"Ordered that the Vacant room in the west end of the Church be made into three convenient pews, and that the Church Wardens agree with some workman to do the same.

"Ordered that Mr. John Custis be removed into the Pew appropriated to the Surveyor General."

Old Orders as to Location and Use of the Galleries

Provision Made for College Students.

On the 10th July, 1718, "whereas complaint had been made to this Vestry, that there was not room in the gallery for the Youth that came from the Colledge, and that they were crowded by others, also that several of the Parishioners were crowded, for remedy of which, it is

"Ordered, that liberty shall be given the Colledge to take that part of ye Gallery for the use of the Colledge Youth, as far from the pillar on the south side of the Isle of the Church, to the north side of the Church,[1] also that farther leave be given them to put a door, with a lock and key to it, to the stairs of the said Gallery, and the Sexton to keep the

---

[1] This west gallery subsequently became known as Lord Dunmore's gallery.

key." In this west end gallery sat Peyton Randolph, (1730,) and George Wythe, (1740,) while students at the College of William and Mary.

December, 17, 1720. Mr. John Holloway, having obtained leave of the Governor, is permitted to erect a gallery in the end of the south wing of the Church, at his own charges.

On the 6th July, 1721, "Ordered that a Gallery be built in the south side of the body of the Church, from the Gallery already erected in the west end, unto the edge of the third window, to project six feet, and to be adorned with banisters. And, that the same be appropriated for the boys of this Parish."

On the 9th May, 1744, it is ordered that "the South Gallery to be extended as far as the Corner."

On Sept. 11, 1753, it is "Ordered that half of the South Gallery, near the Pulpit, in the Church in Williamsburg, be appropriated to the use of the College of William and Mary." Here sat Thomas Jefferson, (student 1760-62,) President James Monroe, (student 1775,) Chief Justice John Marshal, (student 1780,) Edmund Randolph, (student 1776,) President John Tyler, (student 1802-07,) and Winfield Scott, (student 1804.)

Novem. 18, 1755, "Ordered that the Revd. and Honorable Commissary Thomas Dawson, the Honorable Jno. Blair, Esqr., Peyton Randolph, Esqr., Benjamin Waller, Esqr., or any three of them, do agree with a person to build a Loft for an Organ in the Church in the City of Williamsburg, and to set up the same. Mr. Peter Pelham is unanimously appointed and Chosen Organist of the Church in the City of Williamsburg."

On the 7th October, 1762, Mr. Benjamin Waller, on behalf of himself and others, was permitted to build a gallery on the north side of the Church.

The gallery in the north wing was used for the servants of the Parish, and was entered by a stairway from the outside.

The Passing of the Old Regime

THE Old Vestry Book closes with the Order of 1769, which has been quoted, relating to the removal of the Old Steeple and the Old Bell. The closing of the book was doubtless due to the agitation springing from the dirturbances which marked the closing years of Virginia's Colonial history. The passing of the Old Bell seemed to toll the death knell of the old Regime. No other Church in Virginia had been so intimately connected with her Colonial history as this. Bruton Church-yard adjoined the Palace Green. Here ministers were the Court preachers of their day. The record, so far as it gives us glimpses into their life and ministry, indicates that they were worthy men and devoted ministers of the Gospel of Christ. They held their commissions from the Lord Bishop of London, and served as ministers of the established Church of England. The time had come when this fact seriously hindered their influence with many among whom they lived. The passions and prejudices of men are generally undiscriminating. They proved so, to a marked degree, in their relation to the Church. Because her ministry and service were considered as of English appointment, rather than as of Divine authority, they came to be despised by those who had come to hate the authority of the English government. Bruton Church was in the very center of this political and social agitation which culminated in the War of Revolution. Supported warmly by many Loyalists, and by some who were not, she became the object of scorn to many who indulged in wholesale denunciation of all things English.

The Church Service in Colonial Days

Before passing from this long ago period of the history of the Church, let us endeavor to bring back an accustomed scene in Bruton Church in Colonial days:

The old bell breaks the stillness of the Sabbath morn. It calls the whole community to the house of prayer. No other bell is heard. There is no other place for worshippers to go, unless they choose to attend some gathering in an humble meeting house where some who do not like the Prayer-book, vestments, or organ music, are wont to meet to worship according to the dictates of their conscience. The community, as a whole, adheres to the established Church. Old fashioned coaches drive up to the gate and, as the door is opened by a liveried footman, the occupants come forth clothed after the last year's fashion of the Court of George the Third. Around the door the colonial Gentry are assembled, clothed in colonial garb. In voices somewhat animated, and with language not always according to the catechism, they are discussing the stamp act, and other usurpations and injustices of the Government. It is a genuine debate, for here forces are very largely divided, and in the crowd are many stout Tories, who are warm in support of the king, and of his representative, his Excellency the Governor. From Raleigh Tavern there comes a group of men who are representatives of the people in the House of Burgesses. Some of them give indication of having been up late the night before. Their faces show very red beneath their flowing wigs of white. They are talking with loud voice and animated gesture. The king finds few advocates among them, and is being roundly abused in a most disloyal way. They calm down as they approach the Church. The Governor's carriage sweeps down the Palace Green and draws up before the door. The service will soon begin. We pass into the Church. In spite of all the care we take, our footsteps resound through the building as we walk down the flag-stone aisle. Passing into a large square pew we close the door and wait. It is difficult to see those in front of us. The pews, we note, were built to encourage reverence rather than observation. There are some things, however, which we can see in spite of the high back pews.

We notice that the men sit on the north side of the Church, and the women on the south, and are informed that it is because the Vestry has so ordered it. Mr. Peter Pelham enters and, ascending the "organ loft," begins to play the new organ recently purchased in England for the Church by order of the House of Burgesses. The students from the College of William and Mary enter, attended by one of the Masters, and file into the gallery assigned to them in the south wing of the Church. Among them are a number of young Indians who are being educated and christianized at the college. When the students have all entered, the gallery door is locked, and the key given to the sexton. There is no chance now for them to escape, no matter how long the parson may preach.

By an outside stairway, leading up to the gallery in the north wing, we see the servants of the parishioners enter, and reverently await the commencement of the service. We are told that many of them are consistent communicants, and that all have been baptized.

The door at the west, leading from the tower, opens, and the minister, who has vested there, enters and, passing down the aisle, enters the chancel at the east end of the Church. The clerk takes his place at the desk below the pulpit, which stands down in the body of the building at the south-east corner of the Church.

And now, even over the high back pews, we can see that something is attracting general attention. The tower door opens, and the Court procession enters, His Excellency, the Governor, passes down the aisle to his pew. It is in the chancel end of the Church, on the north side of the aisle; it is elevated from the floor. A silk canopy hangs over it, and around it in large letters of gold is the Governor's name. The Council of State, and the members of the House of Burgesses, and the Surveyor-General take pews officially assigned. The service begins. The minister reads, and the clerk, and the people who have Prayer Books, respond. The Beadle keeps his eye upon the College youth in particular, and upon the whole congregation in general. There is no disturbance. We hear what sounds like an imprecation from a near-by pew when the prayer is said for George the Third and the Royal Family, but it is discreetly suppressed, and no note is taken of it.

The service ended, the minister leaves the chancel and, passing down the aisle with the Governor's pew on his right, ascends the high steps leading up into the south-east corner pulpit, takes his text, and begins his sermon. Those who have brought braziers with which to warm their pews, listen with comfort, if not always with patience. Others grow cold and restless, and determine that they would not come to Church if the law had not made it an offence for fine and imprisonment to stay away.

The benediction said, groups gather in the Church (in a very unchurchly way) and exchange greetings, collect the news, discuss the sermon, and exchange opinions, and go to their homes,—homes noted for hospitality and good-cheer, but pervaded nevertheless by a respect for religion and, in many instances, by a beautiful spirit of earnest Christian devotion.

We can find no statement as to the status of the Church during the Revolution. The Revd. John Bracken's rectorship covered this period, as it extended from 1773 to 1818. The house occupied by General Washington while his headquarters were in Williamsburg during the war, was the residence of Chancellor Wythe, which immediately adjoins the Church yard. During this time, he and his staff officers doubtless regularly attended the services of the Church.

The war of the Revolution, which so completely changed political, social, and ecclesiastical conditions, left the old Church unharmed.

"One generation passeth away, another generation cometh," but time, and the vicissitudes of war, have spared the old Church to stand,

"A link among the days, to knit
The generations each to each."

The Church Viewed from the Duke of Gloucester Street

The Church after the Revolution

BRUTON Church suffered, temporarily, as did the whole Episcopal Church in this country, by the disestablishment. Some of the clergy had espoused the cause of the mother country to which they felt bound by their oath of allegiance. Mr. R. S. Thomas, of Smithfield, Va., formerly historiographer of the Diocese of Southern Virginia, has, however, established the fact, from the old records, that the large majority of the Virginia clergy espoused the cause of the colonies in the struggle for independence. Revd. Dr. Madison, President of William and Mary College, and Revd. Mr. Bracken, then rector of Bruton Church, "were avowed and decided partisans of the Colonies."[1] "The Mercers, Harrisons, and Randolphs, and a number of other prominent families,"[1] connected with Bruton Church, had also espoused the cause of independence. But the majority of the people were antagonistic to the Church. The Church was now separated from the state upon which it had leaned for support. It had to adjust itself to new conditions under peculiar difficulties. War had impoverished those who were disposed to support it. On every side the Church was opposed. Her independence of State aid and State control, and her desperate struggle for life in the face of violent opposition, ultimately proved a great blessing to her life. But for a while her faith was tested, and her strength sorely tried. A brief outline of the history of the attack made upon the Episcopal Church is given here as it explains the loss of the glebe lands of Bruton Church.

On the first of January, 1777, the Episcopal Church in Virginia was incorporated, and by the act of incorporation her property was secured. This security was short-

---

[1] Hawks. *Ecclesiastical History, Virginia*, p. 137.

lived. By reason of bitter and persistent opposition, which need not be described here, this act was repealed January 9, 1787;[1] and on the 24th day of January, 1799, an act was passed, "whereby every act which had been passed since the Revolution, touching the Church and its property, was repealed.[2] During this controversy, the Church, fore-seeing the ultimate purpose of this influence which was being brought upon the Legislature, secured learned counsel to examine and report on the legality of the claim of the Protestant Episcopal Church to the tenure of the glebes, Churches, etc. These lawyers reported to the Convention held in Richmond in 1797 that it was their opinion: "That the Protestant Episcopal Church is the exclusive owner of these glebes, Churches, etc." This report was signed by Bushrod Washington, Edmund Randolph, and John Wickham.[3]

The enemies of the Church, having influenced the Legislature to pass the law of 1799, now found it easy to strike the final blow. This was done through an act passed on Jan. 12th, 1802, "by virtue of which the glebe lands were ordered to be sold for the benefit of the public."[4]

The Convention of Virginia authorized Bishop Madison to take the case into the Court of Appeals. This was done in 1804. This case was decided by a vote of three against one in favor of the Episcopal Church. But on the night preceding the day when the opinion was to have been pronounced, Judge Pendleton died.

Judge Tucker was appointed to succeed him, and the case was again argued. Upon the second hearing the court was equally divided, Judge Fleming, who favored the Church, having in each instance refused to sit on the case because he considered himself interested in the decision. The decree of Chancellor Wythe, from which the appeal

---

[1] *Journal of House of Delegates*, p. 87, and *Journal of Senate*, p. 91. Hawks 194.
[2] *Laws of Virginia*, edition 1803, p. 338. Hawks, p. 233. [3] *Virginia Convention Journal* 1797. [4] Hawks, p. 233.

had been taken, was thus affirmed,[1] and the glebe lands of Bruton Church, with those of many other Virginia Churches, were sold.

Early Episcopal Visitations

The first Episcopal visitation ever made to Bruton Church was that of Rt. Revd. Dr. Madison, reported by him to the Convention of 1793. Bishop Moore reports visitations to Bruton Church to the Conventions of 1816, 1819, 1820, 1825 and 1828; and Bishop Meade reports visitations to this Church to the Conventions of 1832 and 1834; but in all these reports there is no mention made of the consecration of Bruton Church. Frequent mention is made in the Convention journals of Churches consecrated, but they seem to have been either new churches, or old ones which had been in disuse, or which had been restored, or extensively repaired. This fact is frequently distinctly stated. The other Churches were doubtless considered as having been consecrated by uninterrupted use in the service of God, or as having remained unharmed and hallowed during the period of their silence. Bruton Church has always been officially called by the Parish name.

Bruton Church made valuable contribution to the work of reconstructing the Church in Virginia, subsequent to the revolution. The Rev. John Bracken was elected rector of the Church in 1773. An examination of the journals of the conventions of the Episcopal Church in Virginia from 1785 to 1818 shows that he was prominent and influential in the councils of the church. In 1785 it is "Ordered, That the thanks of the convention be given to the Rev. John Bracken, for the excellent sermon preached by him this morning."[2] Mr. John Blair was the Lay Deputy to this convention. In 1786

---

[1] Hawks. *Ecclesiastical History, Virginia*, pp. 237-239.
[2] *Journals* of the Convention of Virginia, 1785.

Rev. Mr. Bracken appears as a member of the committee on the Articles of Religion; and at this convention he received nine votes for delegate to the General Convention, "To be holden in Philadelphia." In 1787 he appears as a member of the committee to revise the Canons of the Church. He was elected president of the convention in 1789, to which Mr. Robert Andrews was Lay Deputy from Bruton Church. Mr. Andrews appears as secretary of the convention from 1791-97, when he was succeeded in this office by Rev. John Bracken, D.D. At this convention of 1789, Edmund Randolph, of Bruton Parish, was elected a member of the Standing Committee of the Church, on which Rev Dr. Bracken was placed in 1790. In 1791, and again in 1812, he was appointed delegate to the General Convention of the Church. In 1812, after having been thanked by the convention for his excellent sermon preached at the opening session, he was elected Bishop of the Diocese, receiving twenty-two of the twenty-five votes cast. He resigned the election in 1813.[1]

In 1821 the Rev. Reuel Keith, D. D., of Georgetown, D. C., became Rector of the Church. He reported to the convention, held in Norfolk on the 17th of May, 1821, that there were twenty-five communicants, at that time, in Bruton Church.[2] Dr. Keith remained as rector until 1824, when he was elected Professor in The Theological Seminary, Alexandria.[2]

In 1826 the Rev. William H. Wilmer, D. D., of St. Paul's Church, Alexandria, was elected rector of Bruton Church, and President of William and Mary College.[3]
To the convention of 1827, held in Fredericksburg, Virginia, he made the following report:

"The rector of Bruton Parish, Williamsburg, reports that the condition of the church under his charge is somewhat improving. The building has been repaired—the

---

[1] *Journals* of the Convention of Virginia, 1785-1813.
[2] *Journals* of Convention of Virginia, 1821, 1824.
[3] *Journals* of Convention of Virginia, 1826.

Historical Notes

congregation attend regularly upon public worship. An increasing attention to the order and services of the church is manifested, and the hope is entertained that the pure religion of Jesus Christ is gaining ground. A kind feeling towards the church prevails among the various denominations of Christians, and the rector deems it a matter of advantage to the church, as well as of duty and inclination, to cherish and reciprocate this catholic spirit. There is a flourishing Sunday School attached to the congregation, consisting of one hundred and fifteen scholars, which does honour to the zeal and piety of its teachers.

The number of communicants belonging to the church is about thirty, ten of whom have been added lately. Baptisms twelve; marriages ten; funerals three."[1]

Revd. Dr. Wilmer was a man of beautiful Christian character. The high esteem in which he was held is shown in the tribute paid to his memory by Bishop Moore, who spoke of him to his convention in 1828 as follows: "In touching on the subject of the bereavement we have experienced in the death of our beloved Wilmer, it is impossible for me to find language sufficiently strong to express that sense of his loss which fills my mind. He was one of those who first called my attention to this Diocese, and of the three clergymen who corresponded with me on that subject, one only now remains.

To the usefulness of Dr. Wilmer we must all subscribe. He was a man of business and of piety. He loved his God, and the interest of the Church was near his heart. As a preacher he was faithful, energetic, eloquent. He was the friend of evangelical religion, and considered that the strictest regard to the public order of the Church was perfectly compatible with the most animated social worship, in the houses of his parishioners and friends. His private meetings formed, in his opinion, the nursery of the Church, and were blessed to the edification and comfort of his congregation. He was always ready to discharge his duty.

---
[1] *Journals of Convention of Virginia*, 1827.

Like the Apostle Paul, he not only taught his people publicly, but went from house to house, exhorting them to prepare to meet their God. His fidelity in the discharge of his duty met my warmest approbation; and if it is your wish, my brethren of the clergy, to give an account of your stewardship with joy, oh, let me entreat you all to "go and do likewise."

That he was loved and revered by his people, and by the whole community, is evidenced by the inscription upon the mural tablet placed in the Church to his memory. This inscription is given further on in the book.

In 1828[1] the Rev. Adam Empie was elected rector of the church. He reported to the convention, held in Petersburg that year, that "The whole number of communicants in Bruton Parish, Williamsburg, is 38; that the adult members of the church are about 140; children 100; catechumens 50. The Sunday School consists, at present, of 93; the rector delivers one weekly lecture in the church, which is well attended.

Signed,   A. EMPIE."

In 1829[1] Dr. Empie reports continuous improvement in the church; and to the convention of 1831 he states that the present number of communicants is sixty,[1] and that the number of adults was 109, a mistake, he asserts, having been made in the number reported in 1828.

---

[1] Virginia Convention *Journals*.

The Later Vestry Book

THE next Vestry Book of Bruton Parish opens in 1827, with the following members of the Vestry:

Henry Edloe, Jesse Cole, John Page, Dr. Peachy, Dr. Griffin, W. W. Webb, James Semple, Sr., Robt. McCandlish, Burwell Bassett, William Waller, Leonard Henley and Ferdinand S. Campbell.

Modern Innovations

On April 18, 1829, it was resolved: That a Committee be appointed to ascertain the probable cost of cutting down and painting the pews; and on June 12, 1829 it was "found it would cost about $120," and it was resolved: "That the pews shall be cut down and painted and the Church whitewashed." On Oct. 20, 1829, the Committee appointed to have the pews cut down and painted, and the Church whitewashed, reported that they had done so, and that the expenses thereof amounted to upwards of $200, and that they had only been able to obtain from subscriptions about $120, to defray the expense.

On April 2, 1834, on motion it was "Resolved: That the standing Committee be directed to have the steps and entry at East end of the Church on the outside taken down, and in lieu thereof new steps inside of the Church be made to ascend the Gallery in the East of it."

On the 28th of Feb., 1834, it is "Resolved: That the Rt. Rev. Bishop Moore be respectfully solicited to lay before the Vestry of Trinity Church, New York, the decayed condition of the Church and the poverty of the Parishioners of Bruton Parish, and to use his good offices to procure such aid as their benevolence may prompt."

A Universalist Minister Applies to Preach

On July 7th, 1834, the Vestry took into consideration the application for the Rev. Mr. Skinner, a Universalist Minister, to preach in this Church, and after thorough examination of the said application rejected it.

Old Organ Sold

On April 23rd, 1835, it was Resolved, That the remains of the old organ be given to Mrs. Galt to be disposed of by her in such manner as she may deem proper, the proceeds to be applied to the ornament or improvement of the organ gallery, or such other uses in the Church as she may think expedient.

The items above mentioned all appear during the rectorship of Revd. Dr. Empie.

On Tuesday, May 8th, 1838, during the rectorship of the Rev. William Hodges, a communication was received by the Vestry from the Ladies' Working Society stating that "the Directors and Managers of the same, tender to the Vestry $700, being the proceeds of the late Fair for the repairs of the Church."

On the 19th, of July, 1839, it was "Resolved: That all the interior of the Church not necessary for further use be sold (by the Committee appointed to have the Church repaired) at such time and in such manner as they may deem best.

Interior Remodeled

Acting under these orders, and others of like purport, the Church was remodeled in the interior. The exterior remained unchanged. A partition wall was built across the Church, changing the shape from a cross to a **T**. The chancel was removed from the East end of the Church, where it had been for one hundred and twenty-five years,

INTERIOR VIEW, 1840-1886.

THE DUKE OF GLOUCESTER STREET.

and built out from the newly erected partition wall in the West. The old nave of the Church was not sold, but was afterward used for the Sunday School. The Church, thus turned around, was fancifully decorated on the interior. The old pulpit and the flag stone aisle were removed, and the tower was converted into a place for holding coal.

The diagram on page 58 will show the nature and effect of these alterations of 1840.

The Mayor's Pew

The pew set apart for the Colonial Governor was assigned after the revolution to the Mayor of the City of Williamsburg, out of respect for his position and authority. In 1825 it was occupied by Mr. Wm. T. Galt, who, while Mayor of the city, officially received and welcomed La Fayette when he visited the place.[1]

The pew occupied by the Colonial Governors has been designated in diagram on page 58 as located at the northeast corner of the Church Governor John Page is known to have occupied the pew located at this corner facing south. Mr. Wm. T. Galt and Mr. Robt. Saunders,[2] both mayors of Williamsburg, are known to have occupied the pew intersecting Governor Page's pew just at the corner and facing East, before the change of 1840, and subsequently facing West. The Colonial Governor doubtless occupied a large square pew, which would have embraced them both, and enabled him to sit just opposite the corner pulpit located at the south-east corner, or, by sitting on the other side of the pew, to face the Chancel in the East. There are letters extant which locate these as the pews of the above named persons; and there is one person[3] still living who remembers the red canopy hanging there which originally marked the pew of the Colonial Governor. In 1704 the Governor occupied a pew on the south side of the Chancel. (See p. 42).

---

[1] From an old letter. [2] Mrs. Robt. Saunders was the daughter of Governor John Page. [3] Mrs. Randolph Harrison.

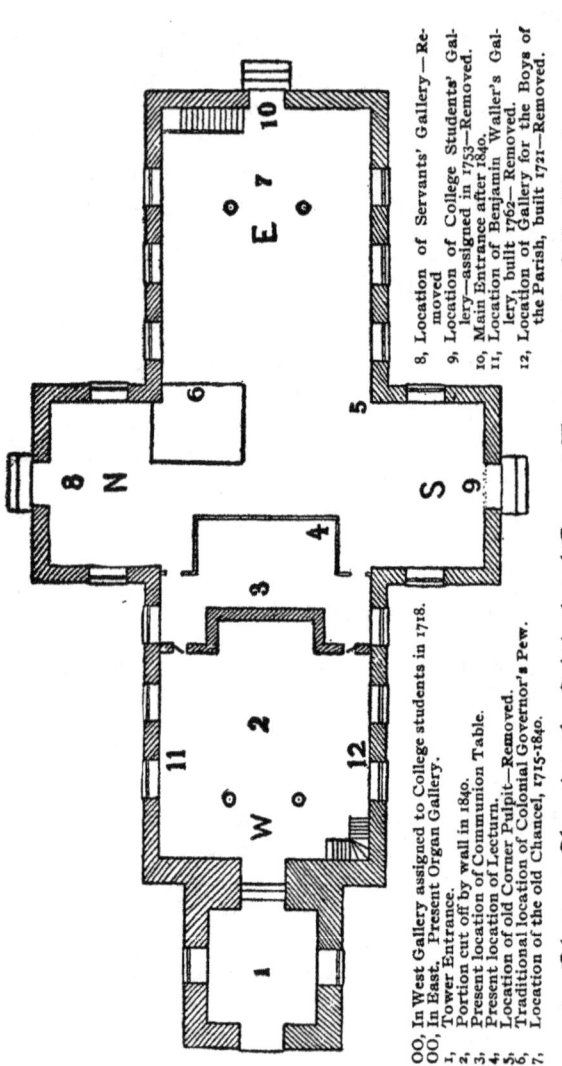

OO, In West Gallery assigned to College students in 1718.
OO, In East, Present Organ Gallery.
1, Tower Entrance.
2, Portion cut off by wall in 1840.
3, Present location of Communion Table.
4, Present location of Lecturn.
5, Location of old Corner Pulpit—Removed.
6, Traditional location of Colonial Governor's Pew.
7, Location of the old Chancel, 1715-1840.
8, Location of Servants' Gallery—Removed.
9, Location of College Students' Gallery—assigned in 1753—Removed.
10, Main Entrance after 1840.
11, Location of Benjamin Waller's Gallery, built 1762—Removed.
12, Location of Gallery for the Boys of the Parish, built 1721—Removed.

Diagram Showing the Original and Present Arrangement of the Church

The Pews Rented Out

On the 22d day of May 1840, in order to obtain revenue, it was resolved, that the pews of the Church be rented out; and on the 22d day of May, 1840, there appears the following record:

No. 5, to Miss B. Page, twenty dollars; No. 6, to Mrs. Coleman, twenty-five dollars; No. 7, to Richard Randolph, twenty-five dollars; No. 8, to Dickie Galt, thirty dollars; No. 9, to H. A. Burwell, thirty dollars; No. 11, to John Coke, thirty dollars; No. 12, to A. G. Southall, thirty-two dollars and fifty cents; No. 13, to William Martin, thirty dollars; No. 14, to R. P. Waller, forty-two dollars; No. 15, to A. D. Galt, twenty dollars; No. 16, to Ro. P. Waller, thirty-three dollars, No. 17, to G. Durfey, twenty-five dollars; No. 18, to W. W. Vest, twenty-five dollars; No. 19, to W. W. Tyler, fifteen dollars, No. 20, to S. S. Griffin, fifteen dollars; No. 21, to Robert Anderson, forty dollars; No. 22, to Robert Anderson, forty dollars; No. 23, to Tho. R. Dew, fifty dollars; No. 24, to Robert Anderson, fifty dollars; No. 25, to B. Tucker, fifty dollars; No. 26, to Ro. Saunders, fifty dollars; No. 27, to John B. Christian, forty dollars; No. 28, to Jesse Cole, forty dollars; No. 29, to Sam. F. Bright, forty dollars; No. 30, to R. M. Garrett, forty-five dollars; No. 31, to Thos. G. Peachy, forty dollars; No. 32, to J. C. Sheldon, fifty dollars; No. 33, to Dabney Browne, forty dollars; No. 34, to Robert McCandlish, sixty dollars; No. 35, to Moreau Bowers, thirty-seven dollars; No. 36, to William H. Pierce, forty dollars; No. 37, to Benjamin Hansford, thirty dollars; No. 38, to Lucius F. Cary, forty dollars; No. 39, to John Millington, thirty-four dollars; No. 40, to William Edloe, thirty-six dollars; No. 41, to John M. Galt, twenty-two dollars; No. 42, to Mrs. Mary Shield, twenty-four dollars; No. 43, to Henley Taylor, fifteen dollars; No. 44, to Mrs. Henry Edloe, twenty dollars; No. 45, to John Tyler, fifteen dollars; No. 46, to Mrs. Mary Carter, ten dollars; No. 48, to Mrs. Miller, ten dollars.

At a meeting of the vestry held Jan. 23rd, 1878, it was "Resolved, That the pews in this Church are free and all persons are invited to attend our services."

Town Clock Placed in Church Steeple

On the 14th day of July, 1840, on motion, it was Resolved, That the Town authorities have permission to have the town clock removed to the Church and fixed up therein.

"At a meeting of the vestry held on the 8th of May, 1841, it was "Resolved, That the Church be fitted up in the usual emblems of mourning on Friday the 14th day of May, in compliance with the recommendation of the President of the United States, because of our national bereavement in the recent death of Wm. Henry Harrison, our late President."

The Revd. William Hodges, D. D., resigned in 1848, and was succeeded by the Revd. Henry M. Denison, who continued rector until March, 1850. He was again elected rector in 1852. He was succeeded in 1856 by the Revd. Geo. Wilmer, D. D., who was rector for one year. Dr. Wilmer was followed in the rectorship by Revd. Thomas Ambler, who served as rector for twelve years, from 1860 to 1872.

On the 1st day of May, 1852, "On motion it was resolved, That a Gallery be erected, and that Dr. Jno. M. Galt and Mr. G. Durfey be appointed a Committee to draft a plan and to let the same to the lowest bidder."

The last entry in the Vestry book, preceding the Civil War, was made on April 13, 1853, at which time the following gentlemen were enrolled as Vestrymen:

Robert Saunders, Goodrich Durfey, Robert T. Cole, M. Galt, R. M. Garrett, C. Jos. Coleman, Turner Christian, W. W. Vest, John A. Henley, Joshua Walker, Jr., William Waller, Robert McCandlish.

Historical Notes

The Revd. Thos. M. Ambler, who was Rector of the Church during the time of the Civil War, states that one year after the battle of Williamsburg, some if not all of the Communion silver of the Church was removed from the city, and taken by him to South Carolina and elsewhere, and brought back by him at the conclusion of the war.

He further states that no service was held in the Church during the war because the authorities would not allow the service unless the prayer for the President of the United States was said. During a part of this time the Church was used as a hospital for the Confederate soldiers. The services, however, were not abandoned, for Revd. Mr. Ambler held regular services on Sunday at his home, which continued until he left the city to enter the army as a commissioned Chaplain. After the war he returned as rector, and visited the north, securing $250 for repairing the roof of the Church.

The first entry in the Vestry book after the Civil War was made on October, 1865, at which time the following gentlemen were enrolled:

Revd. Thos. M. Ambler, Rector; Mr. Robert Saunders, Mr. P. Montague Thompson, Mr. W. W. Vest, Mr. R. F. Cole, Mr. J. C. Munford, Mr. E. Taliaferro, Mr. Richard Hansford, Mr. G. Durfey, Mr. Wm. S. Peachy, Mr. John A. Henley, Dr. Robert Garrett.

After the rectorship of Revd. Thos. M. Ambler, the Revd. Geo. Wilmer, D. D., was for the second time elected rector in 1872, and served four years. The Revd. Jaquelin Meredith served as rector from 1876 to 1877; Revd. Henry Wall, S. D. T., from 1877 to 1880; Revd. Alexander Overby from 1880 to 1885; the Revd. F. G. Burch from 1885 to 1887; The Revd. Lyman B. Wharton, D. D , now Professor of Latin in the College of William and Mary, was rector in 1888; The Revd. T. C. Page served as rector from 1889 to 1893; and the Revd. William T. Roberts from 1894 to 1902.

At a meeting of the vestry of the Bruton Parish held in the lecture room on Monday, the 5th of April, 1873, on motion it was "Resolved, That the rector, Revd. George T. Wilmer, is hereby requested to furnish any information in his possession relative to any of the missing records of this Parish, or their contents, and report at his convenience to the Vestry.

At a vestry meeting held on October 27, 1885, it was "Resolved, That a committee appointed be authorized and empowered to contract to have a tin roof put upon the Church."

"At a meeting of the vestry of Christ Church,* Bruton Parish, held on March 2nd, 1886, the Revd. Francis M. Burch, Rector, being present, it was determined: First, to repair the floor and make it perfectly secure; second, that the walls should be plastered and kalsomined; third, that the side lamps should be removed, and the Church lighted by chandeliers; fourth, that the present Pulpit (see illustration showing interior view 1840-1886,) be taken down, and reading desk and Pulpit and Communion table supplied; fifth, that the Gallery in the north end of the Church be removed."

For these, and other repairs, the "Catharine Memorial Society" placed $300 in the treasury of the Church. The changes determined upon were made, and the furniture for the chancel purchased. The pulpit purchased by this Society was subsequently presented to St. John's Church, Petersburg, Va.

On March 24, 1887, the vestry granted the request of "The Catharine Memorial Society to repair the old monuments in the church yard, and otherwise to put in order as their means would justify."

On February 12th, 1902, "the rector, Revd. W. T. Roberts, reported that the deed to the Parish house had been made in the name of the trustees of the Church, and

---

* We occasionally, at this time, find Bruton Church thus designated, without authority.

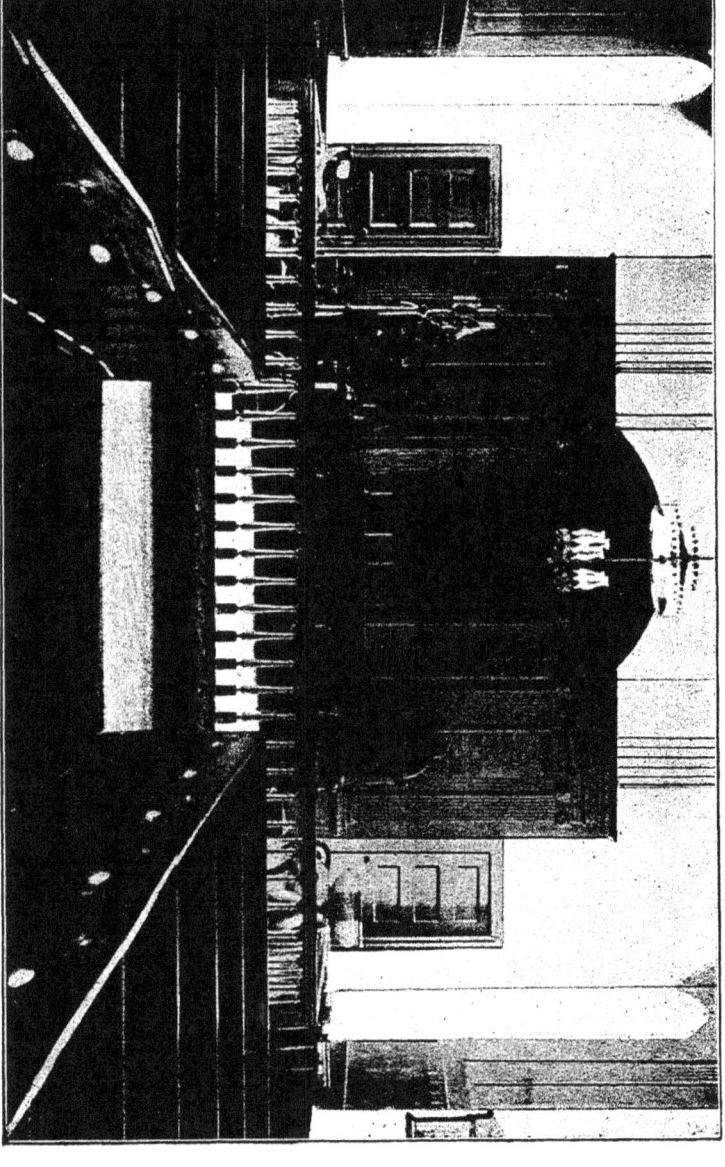

The Interior View of the Church, 1886-1903.

had been recorded." This Parish house was secured in order to make room for the Sunday School and Parish meetings, in view of the restoration of the Church which was then contemplated.

The Restoration of the Church

It has long been thought that the comparatively modern changes which were made in the Church in 1840, destroying its ancient cruciform shape, were out of keeping with the rest of the building; and that the interior of the Church should be restored to its ancient form.

The following account of the action of the congregation and Vestry, which appeared in the Southern Churchman of May 30, 1903, will show what has been determined upon in this matter:

"At a meeting of the vestry of Bruton Church, held Saturday evening, May 23rd, the rector, the Revd. W. A. R. Goodwin, stated that he had, at the request of the vestry, presented the question of the restoration of the Church to the congregation on Sunday morning, May 19th, and asked that those opposed to such restoration, if any, should so inform the rector, and that at the service held May 17, 8 P. M., at the visitation of the Bishop, the rector had stated that final action on this matter would be taken by the vestry on May 23d; that no member of the congregation had offered any opposition to the plan, but that a great many had expressed their hearty approval of the undertaking.

Mr. Mercer moved, that whereas no objection had come to the knowledge of the vestry on the part of any member of the congregation to the proposed restoration of the Church edifice, therefore, be it

Resolved, That the vestry proceed with the consideration of the restoration proposed by Dr. Garrett at the meeting of the vestry, held May 8, 1903, which is in the following words, to-wit:

"Resolved, That it is the sense of the vestry to restore Bruton Church to its original form, provided the move on their part meets with the approval of a majority of the members of the Church, and that the rector be requested to present this matter to the congregation and ascertain their views on the subject, and to report to the vestry at some future meeting."

It is further provided that no steps in this matter shall be taken until the necessary funds have been received. This was unanimously carried.

Dr. Garrett thereupon moved that the vestry proceed to take such steps as shall be necessary to restore Bruton Church to its original form; provided, however, that no work shall be undertaken until the necessary funds shall have been secured, and the rector is hereby authorized to solicit contributions for this purpose, and that all funds collected for this object be turned over to the treasurer of the Church and be deposited in bank on interest-bearing account. Unanimously adopted.

The rector suggested that the vestry associate with themselves, in the restoration of the Church, an advisory committee, consisting of the Rt. Revd. A. M. Randolph, Revd. Dr. B. D. Tucker, Diocese of Southern Virginia; Revd. J. J. Gravatt, Diocese of Virginia; Revd. Dr. Randolph H. McKim, Washington, D. C.; Revd. Dr. William R. Huntington, Diocese of New York; Mr. J. Frederick Kernachan, New York, and such others as they may deem proper. This suggestion was unanimously agreed to.

It is gratifying to the vestry to be able to say that after a full and free discussion of the proposed restoration of the dear old Church, not only in the sessions of the vestry, and among the congregation, but with many distinguished visitors, we are yet to hear of any serious opposition on the part of any one, and we are assured that the funds necessary to make the changes contemplated will soon be available. We have already some substantial promises of aid." H. D. COLE,
Registrar of the Vestry.

Historical Notes 65

The experience and knowledge of the gentlemen associated with us on the advisory committee will be of great service to the vestry in the undertaking, and will give to the Church at large the assurance that the work will be wisely planned and executed.

In Memoriam

GOD, through nature, has done much to make beautiful the spacious grounds where the old Church stands. Each season gives to the place a special charm, and a varied loveliness. The spring calls forth the wild butter-cups which spread themselves over the entire grounds like a rich cloth of gold. The summer breathes upon the roses which blossom forth and bloom here among the tombs and above the green graves of the dead of other days. The ancient trees, full-leaved, cast upon the dark walls of the old Church deep shadows which lengthen and deepen with the dying day. Then the touch of autumn tells that another year is beginning to die. The berries redden on the English hawthorn tree which stands near by the ancient tower door; the vine, clinging to the north wall of the Church, turns crimson; and the leaves flush with varied color, then fall and die. In the bleak winter the wind, as if at requiem, sighs through the bare trees, and moans about the walls and tower of the old Church. Only the ivy which mantles the eastern end of the building, and clings to the old trees in the Church yard, remains green. But the scene is one of matchless beauty, when, from heaven, the mantle of spotless white softly falls o'er Church, and tombs, and bending trees. And then, again, there come the glad days that speak of life, and suggest thoughts of immortality. Dormant vital forces stir and breathe and move. The air is filled with the music of birds singing as they nest in the trees in the Temple court, and is ladened with the perfume of the hawthorn bloom, and violets come forth and weave a border of purple and green about the bases of the tombs.

Through the many changing seasons, unchanged the Church has stood. The touch of time has been gentle and forbearing. Through widening cracks the old Church, at times, has made mute appeals for protecting care, to which those who loved her have responded. The ancient tower, through which so many of the living and the dead have passed, is even now appealing for repairs to protect its strength. What time has spared so long and hallowed, must not suffer harm from man's neglect. To secure its protection and preservation the Church should be ENDOWED. This endowment should be given, not to maintain the living service, which it is the privilege of those who worship here to do, but to provide a perpetual fund for the preservation of the old Church building, and for the rightful care of the grounds where sleep the dead who worshipped here, and loved, as we do now, this sacred soil which now enshrines their dust. This endowment would be a fitting tribute from the living to the memory of the dead, and would be to the glory of God Who has watched over and protected this ancient and hallowed Temple which bears witness to the faith and devotion of our fore-fathers.

Communion Silver

THE Church has at present three sets of Communion Silver, which on account of their sacred associations and antiquity are highly prized and carefully preserved. The following description of this plate is taken from a book entitled "Old Plate," by John H. Buck, published by the Gorham Manufacturing Co., New York, 1888, pp. 210-212:

The Jamestown Church Service

"CHALICE, H 10¾ in. PATEN, Dia 7 in. One mark, **I W,** oval object below, plain shield.

Inscription on each: **Mixe not holy thinges with profane. Ex dono francisci Morrison, Armigeri* Anno Domi 1661.** This maker's mark is on the celebrated cup formerly belonging to the Blacksmith's Company, London, 1655, and purchased at the Dexter sale for no less a sum than £378, and it is also found in a shaped shield on the copper plate preserved at Goldsmith's Hall 1675-1697.

ALMS BASIN, Dia 9¾ in. Four marks: 1, Lion passant; 2, Leopard's Head, crowned; 3, Small Roman a,[1] London 1739: 4, maker's mark, .T F. (Thomas Farren). Inscription: **for the use of James City Parish Church.** This service has been in use in Bruton Church since the Church at Jamestown was abandoned. (See illustration.)

Bruton Parish Church

Two-handled CUP AND COVER, gilt H 3¾ in.; Dia. 4¼ in. Four marks: Lion passant; 2, Leopard's Head, crowned; 3, black letter small **i** London 1686; 4, maker's mark **P • H,** crown and two ermine spots above, crescent below, shaped escutcheon, Peeter Harache. This maker's

---

*Francis Morrison was at this time acting Governor of the Colony.

[1] This should be small Roman d, London, 1739.

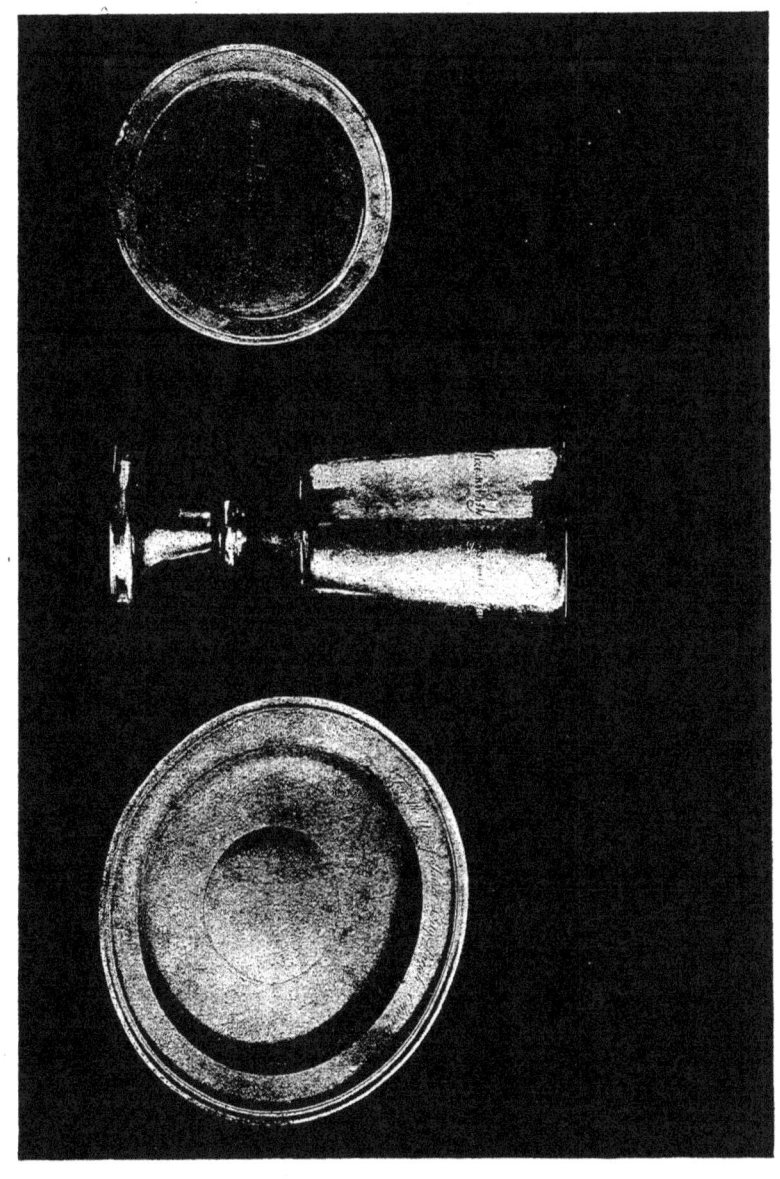

The Jamestown Communion Service.

Historical Notes

mark is also to be found on the copper plate preserved at Goldsmith's Hall.

PATEN, Dia 5½ in. Four marks: 1, Lion passant; 2, Leopard's Head, crowned; 3, small Roman b,[1] London 1737; 4, maker's mark **R•G** with **C** above and **C** below. (Richard Gurney and Co.)

The cup is beautifully chased and embellished with applique leaves and bears private arms, the Paten is of less delicate workmanship. (See illustration.)

[The following letter in reference to the two-handled cup and cover written recently is inserted here, as it contains additional information in regard to this silver which has been commonly known as the Queen Anne Service.]

> 49 North 8th Ave., Mount Vernon, N. Y.,
> October 21, 1903.

Revd. Sir:—

The Gorham Co. have handed me your favor of the 17th inst., to reply to. You are welcome to use the required matter from "Old Plate," as you suggest. In 1897 I received a letter from the President of William and Mary College[2] with regard to the cup and cover now in use in your church. "I have a letter of Samuel Athaires from London to the President and Masters of the college, under date 29th July, 1775, in which it is stated that he has in his custody 'the gilt sacramental cup and patten, together with the bible which was left by Lady Gooch to the college of William and Mary, and which, when the times would permit he would send addressed to the Bursar of that seminary.' Now Lady Gooch was Rebecca, daughter of William Stanton, Esq." (the arms on the dexter side of shield engraved on cup are those of Stanton). "I suppose the cup and bible fell into the custody of the church through Revd. John Bracken, who was president

---

[1] The letter on the paten is a small Roman q, London, 1751.
[2] Lyon G. Tyler, M. A., LL. D.

of the college in 1812, and also minister of Bruton Church.

Yours very truly,

JOHN H. BUCK.

The King George Service

FLAGON, H 10½ in. CHALICE, H 10 in. ALMS BASIN, Dia 10 in. Four marks on Flagon: 1, Lion passant; 2, Leopard's Head, crowned; 3, Old English capital L[1] London 1766; 4, maker's mark *T.H.* crowned (Thos. Heming).

On Chalice the maker's mark is wanting, and the date letter is an old Old English I, London 1764, there are no marks on the Alms Basin. All engraved with the Royal Arms between the initials G III R with motto "Honi soit qui mal y pense."

Plate of the same date and by the same maker is at Trinity Church, New York." (See illustration.)

These services of communion silver, when not in use, are kept in a fire-proof vault in a building of the Eastern State Hospital.

The Font

According to tradition the Font in Bruton Church was used in the Church at Jamestown, and was brought from that place when the House of Burgesses was moved to Williamsburg, in 1699.

FONT STONES

In the Calendar of State Papers Vol. I, page 35, there is the following record relating to the importation of Font Stones:

"One order more, same date (April 19, 1692), concerning font stones at Tindall's Point, Mr. Robt. Read one,

---

[1] This old English L is not exactly the same form as the style of L on the silver.

THE KING GEORGE III COMMUNION SERVICE.

Capt. Thorp one, & by Capt. Thorp's Information to my Under Sherif, Capt. ffra, Page one, Capt. James Archer, one & y^t ye Stone in Broughton, p'ifh Church is ye fame, & y^t Capt. Page gave his Receipt for them, but to whome he Knows not."

The tradition in the Parish is that when the Jamestown font was brought to Williamsburg, the one imported in 1692 was given to one of the neighboring Churches.

The Bell

The bell which has rung out the years for more than a century and a quarter, has engraved upon it: "The gift of James Tarpley to Bruton Parish, 1761." There was a still older bell, which has been referred to, for the vestry, in 1769, entered an order for their contractor, Benjamin Powell, to have the "Old Bell and the materials of the old steeple." The ancient clock still looks down from the steeple, but for many years it has been unmindful of the flight of time.

Old Record Books

The old Parish Register of the Church is still in the possession of the Vestry. It was found some years ago in a box of papers where it had doubtless been hid for safe keeping during the war. During this time it was badly mutilated by some person, ignorant of its value. A large number of pages were torn from the front and back of the book. It now contains the records of Baptisms from 1739 to May 21st, 1797, and the record of Deaths from April 13th, 1662, to December 18th, 1761. Thus it would appear that pages containing the record of seventy-seven years were torn from the front, and pages containing the record of deaths for thirty-six years were torn from the back. The book that remains has been rebound, and is kept in an iron safe.

The entries in this Old Parish register prior to 1674, seem to belong to one of the adjacent churches, probably to the one located in Marston Parish, which was united with Middletown Parish in 1674. The Baptismal record in this book shows with what care the members of the Church provided spiritual ministration for the children of their servants. The illustration given shows two pages of this ancient record.

As stated in the introduction, the old vestry book of the Parish was either lost or destroyed during the wars, or was burned with the house of Revd. John McCabe in Hampton.

Extracts from Sermons Preached in Bruton Church by Commissary Blair, 1710-1743

On Lying and Swearing

"Thus now I have done with my text; but I am afraid I have done no good all this while, and that the evil one, from whom the spirit of lying and swearing comes, will be abundantly too hard for all that I can say or do to fortify you against his devices. Learn, I beseech you, this easy part of Christianity, to be men of your word, and to refrain from the evil custom of swearing; and to refrain from it from a right principle—the fear of God. I know no vice that brings more scandal to our Church of England. The Church may be in danger from many enemies; but perhaps she is not so much in danger from any as from the great number of profane persons that pretend to be of her; enough to make all serious people afraid of our society, and to bring down the judgments of God upon us, for 'by reason of swearing the land mourneth.' But be not deceived: our Church has no principles that lead to swearing more than the dissenters; but, whatever, Church is uppermost, there are always a great many who, having no religion at all, crowd into it and bring it into disgrace and disreputation; but the time is coming that the tares must be separated from the wheat; and they shall be cast with the evil one—the devil that loved them—into hell; but the angels shall carefully gather the wheat into God's barn. If ye know these things, happy are ye if ye do them."

ON THE VANITY OF APPAREL

"I doubt not but it was designed to cast a slur upon the vanity of apparel, since it is a thing of so little estimation in the sight of God that He bestows it in the highest degree on the meanest of his creatures. For it is to be presumed, had it been a thing of any great worth in itself, instead of bestowing these admirable varieties of colors, gildings, and embroideries upon tulips, He would have bestowed them upon creatures of higher dignity. Whereas, on mankind He has bestowed but very sparingly of these gaudy colors and features; a great part of them being black, a great part of them being tauny, and a great part being of other wan and dusky complexions, show that it is not the outward gaudy beauty that He values, but the ornaments of the mind—Christian graces, and virtues—which, in His sight, are of great price."

Appendix

Appendix A

THE following notes give an account of the Induction controversy mentioned on page 23.

"The following from Sir Edward Northy, Knight, her Majesty's (Queen Anne's) Attorney-General for the Colony, given in the preceeding year, opens the case between the Vestry and Mr. Whateley. It is his opinion—

"On consideration of ye Laws of Virginia provision being made by an act Intituled Church to be built or Chapel of Ease, for the building a Church in Each Parish, and by the act intituled Ministers to be Inducted: that Ministers of each Parish shall be inducted On ye presentation of ye Parishioners. And ye Church Wardens being by ye Act, Instituted Church Wardens to keep ye Church in repair, and provide Ornaments, to Collect ye Minister's dues, and by ye act for the better support & maintenance of ye Clergy, provision being made for ye Ministers of ye parishes, and by ye said act for inducting Ministers, ye Governour being to Induct ye Ministers to be presented, and thereby, he being constituted Ordinary and as Bishop of ye Planticon, and with a power to punish Ministers preaching Contrary to ye Law—I am Of Opinion ye Advowson and right of presentation to ye Churches is subject to the Law of England, (there being no express Law of that Plantation made further concerning the same.) Therefore when the Parishioners present thier Clerke, and he is Inducted by ye Governour, (who is to, and must Induct On ye presentation of ye parishioners,) the Incumbent is in for his life, and Cannot be displaced by ye parishioners.—If ye parishioners do not present a Minister to the Governour within six months after any Church shall become Voyd, The Governour as Ordinary shall & may Collate a Clerke to said Church by Law; and his Collatee shall hold ye Church for his life. If ye Parishioners have never presented, they have a reasonable time to present a Minister, but if they will not present, being required so to do, the Governour may also, in their default, Collate a Minister. In inducting Ministers by ye Governour On ye presentation of ye Parish, or on his own Collation, he is to see the Ministers be qualified according as that act for Inducting Ministers requires. In Case of ye Avoydance of any Church, ye Governour, (as Ordinary of ye Plantation) is, according to the statute 28: H 8th, Cap. 11, Sect. 5, to appoint a Minister to Officiate till the Parish shall present one, Or ye six months being lapsed, and such person appointed to officiate in ye Vacancy, is to be paid for his services out of ye profitts thereof from ye time ye Church became Voyd. By the Law above stated in this case, No Minister is to officiate as such till he hath shewed to ye Governour he is qualified according as ye said act directs. If the Vestry do not levie ye tobacco for ye Minister, ye Courts then must decree the same to be levied.

"Edward Northy,
July ye 29th, 1703."

"At a Council held at Williamsburg ye 3d day of March, [1704,] Present, His Excellency in Council.

Upon reading at this Board Sir Edward Northy, Knight, her Majesty's Attorney General, his Opinion upon ye act of Assembly of this Colony, relating to ye Church, and particularly Concerning Induction of Ministers,—His Excellency in Council is pleased to order that a Copy of ye said Sir Edward Northy his opinion be sent to ye Churchwardens of each Parish within this Colony, Requiring them Upon ye receipt thereof forthwith to call a Vestry, & there to cause the same to be read and entered into ye Vestry books, to ye end ye said Vestrys may offer to his Excellency what they think proper thereupon.

"Wm. Robertson, Clerk Council.
"Ff. Nicholson."

"Sir Edward Northy's Opinion being read to ye Vestry, Mr. John Page is requested by them to draw an answer on ye foll: heads.—Being without a Minister, have & shall do our utmost Endeavour to gett one.

"As to ye Right of Presentation and Induction, think it too Weighty a matter for us to handle, but hope ye Worshipfull Assembly Convened will take care for ye Clearing of yt point."

"Mr. Solomon Whately, it seems, was not disposed to submit tamely to be thrust out, and accordingly,

"At a Vestry held ye 22d day of May, 1704, Present
His Excellency,
Mr. Solomon Whateley, Minister,
Col. Phil Ludwell,   Mr. Wm. Pinkethman,
Mr. John Dormer,   Mr. Wm. Hansford,
Capt. Hugh Norwell,   Mr. Joseph White,

"The Petition of Solomon Whateley, Clerke, humbly sheweth to His Excellency ffrancis Nicholson, her Majesty's Lieutenant & Governor General of Virginia.—May it please your Excellency, that upon ye death of Mr. Cope Doyley, late Minister of Bruton Parish, (lying part in ye County of York, and part in ye County of Jamestown,) the Vestry of ye said Parish holding a meeting were pleased (without Your petitioner's seeking to any of them, or so much as knowing of ye Vacancy,) by Common Consent to make ye following Order." Here follows the order made in Vestry 17th Oct., 1702, inviting Mr. Whateley to officiate, & desiring the Governour to give "the same Mr. Whateley leave to remove from ye Parish where he is now entertained, and also to invite ye said Mr. Whateley to take upon him the Cure of this Parish. According to which ye petitioner, with your Excellency's Consent, and also probation given in form and manner as in ye said Order specified, presented himself at Williamsburg, where, to his great surprise, he found ye said Vestry by an unaccountable change of mind in some of them, divided among themselves upon some causeless debate relating to ye said Order; which, however, at last upon your petitioner having been putt to many unnecessary troubles and expenses, at another Vestry holden December ye 13th, 1702, terminated in ye order following:—Sunday, December ye 13th, 1702. Ordered that ye Reverend Mr. Solomon Whateley be entertained Minister of this Parish for One Year, to begin at Christmas next, allowing ye Salary according to Law; in Conformity to which two Orders of Vestry, (though the latter seeming very materially to derogate from ye former,) Your Petitioner at ye time prefixed entered upon ye said Cure, & continued without any lett or impediment to officiate in ye same, faithfully discharging all ye duties and affairs of his place in ye said Parish till the tenth day of ffeb: last past,—when, notwithstanding Your Excellency being then known to be at your own home so neare adjoining to ye Church where the Vestry was held, and being at least one of the Most Considerable Inhabitants of the said Parish, & whose Consent one would have thought might have been as necessarily required to the turning out of the Minister as it was to the taking him in, Yet they were pleased to make ye two Orders following"—

[Here follow the two orders, dismissing Mr. Whateley, after 25th day of March, and authorizing Col. Ludwell to invite the Rev. Mr. Grace to officiate in the Parish.]

"The said Rev. Mr. Grace having indeed received the invitation Mentioned in ye said Order, but (as being a Gentleman newly arrived in this Province, & unacquainted with such kind of proceedings,) reasonably judging it not proper for him to intermeddle in an affair which boare ye aspect of so unlucky a precedent against himself,—May it please yr Excellency, the case standing thus with your petitioner, he could not think it proper for him to seek to provide for himself elsewhere, until he should have first laid ye whole Matter before your Excellency, to whose Inspection (both as Governour and Ordinary within this province) he conceives things of this nature properly to Appertain; without whose Knowledge, therefore, he could not think it in his own power to dispose of himself elsewhere,—to whose disposall, therefore, he entirely submits himself, humbly supplicating your Excellency's favorable regard; and not doubting but that from so Known a Patron of those that serve at ye Altar, he shall obtain what relief You shall in Your Wisdom judge proper and reasonable to be afforded to a person of his profession lying under so sad and disheartening circumstances. Shall Your petitioner (as in duty bound) allways pray for Your Excellency's long life and Prosperity.

Your Excellency's
Most Humble Petitioner
and
Most obedient Servant,
Solomon Whateley."

"The Vestry were in a hard place. Mr. Whateley's letter, which is well conceived, and flatteringly commended to his "Excellency's" consideration, is followed by the one written by Col. Ludwell to the Rev. Mr. Grace, which gentleman, feeling it his duty to conciliate the Governor, had handed Ludwell's epistle to Nicholson. Ludwell to Rev. Mr. Grace:"

"York, ffeby: ye 24, 1704.

Rev. Sir,—I wrote to You about a fortnight past, but having heard nothing from You, I suppose it miscarried. Therefore I send this to acquaint You that the Church of Bruton Parish being Vacant, and the Vestry having heard a good character of you, have desired me to invite You to come and give them a Sermon, in order to your being chosen Minister of that Parish, if they like: I doubt not you will maintain ye character Capt. Humphreys hath given me of you, and should be glad of so good a Guide. I suppose I need not Commend ye Parish to You, since every body can tell You it is one of the best in Virginia. I suppose you also know it is ye Parish wherein Williamsburg stands. I desire to hear from You as soon as maybe. If you please to Cover Your letter to Mr. Charles Chiswell, at ye Secretary's Office, or Walter Cromley, at Dr. Blair's store, in Williamsburg, it will come safe to me.

Your Most Humble Servant,
Phill. Ludwell."

"This letter I received from Coll. Ludwell at Capt.

Royall's house, By what hand it came I know not. Some days after I went to Williamsburgh, and delivered it to ye Governour with my own hands.

Isaac Grace.

May ye 14th, 1704."

"Whereas Coll. Ludwell acquainted the above said Vestry that I sayd, Upon his Invitation to that Parish, I should be glad of so good a one, if I might have it with ye Governour's liking,—I utterly deny I ever said any such thing. The substance of My Answer, to ye best of my remembrance, being, that ye Governour had a knowledge of the matter, and I would not intermeddle in it without his Consent.—Withall returning Coll. Ludwell thanks for his Offer,

Isaac Grace.

May ye 14th, 1704."

"Immediately following, Nicholson orders the record of the instructions sent from England:

"And to ye end ye Ecclesiastical Jurisdiction of ye said Lord Bishop of London may take place in that our Collony, so far as Conveniently may, we do think fit that You do give all Countenance and Encouragement of ye Exercise of ye Same, excepting only ye Collating to Benefices, Granting Lycenses for Marriages and probate of wills, which we have reserved to You our Governour as the Commander in Chief of our said Collony for ye time being.

"The above-written is one of her Majesty's Royal Instructions, bearing date ye 12 day of December, 1702, and sent to

ffr. Nicholson.

"You are not to prefer any Minister to any.... benefit in that our Colony without a Certificate from ye Right Reverend father in God, ye Lord Bishop of London, of his being Conformable to the Doctrine and discipline of ye Church of England, and of a good life and Conversation: and if any person already preferred to a Benefice, shall appear to you to give scandal, either by his Doctrine or Manner, You are to use Your best means for removal of him, and to supply ye Vacancy in such manner as we have directed.

"You are to give Order further (if ye same be not already done) that every orthodox Minister within Your Government be one of ye Vestry in his respective parish, and that no Vestry be held without him, Except in Case of Sickness, or that after Notice of a Vestry Summoned, he omit to come.

"You are to enquire whether there be any Minister within your Government who preaches and administers the Sacraments in any Orthodox Church or Chapell without being in due Orders, and to give an account thereof to ye Lord Bishop of London.

"These are three of her Most Sacred Majesties Royal Instructions, bearing date ye 12th day of December, 1702, and sent to

ffra. Nicholson."

"At a Vestry held ye third day of June, 1704,
  Mr. Wm. Timson, Capt. Hugh Norwell,
  Mr. Wm. Hansford, Mr. Joseph White,
  Coll. Phil. Ludwell, Mr. John Page.
  Mr. John Dorman,

Whereas the foregoing Entry, bearing date ye 22d day of May, 1704, appears on Record as though they were entered by order of Vestry, the Vestrymen therein Mentioned, do declare that the said entrys were not made by Order of the Vestry, but by His Excellency's immediate Command to the Clark. Mr. Solomon Whateley came into the Vestry and made the following Verball proposition to this Vestry, (to wit)—What I have done Is in obedience to his Excellency's Command, & I have never said to any person that I have a right to this Parish, nor do I insist on a right to it.— Mr. Whateley likewise declared he preached by ye Governour's Command.

It being so late in ye day that ye Vestry have not time to consider of what was entere 1 in this Book by his Excellency's Command On ye 22d day of May last, & that of what Mr. Whateley hath now said, It is ordered that ye consideracon thereof be referred to ye Next Vestry."

"The following address from the Vestry to Governor Nicholson was spread upon record at the same meeting:

"May it please Your Excellency—

We have Sir Edward Northy's Opinion before us Concerning ye Right of Presentation and Induction of Ministers, with an order of Council thereupon, by which find some replyes Expected,—but it being a Matter of too great Weight & Consequence for us to determine, Cannot but hope ye Revisall of ye Laws, and ye Worshipful Assembly, have and will take such care as may effectually conduce to ye cloosing those heads and all others in relation to them, to ye future ease and satisfaction of all. And to the end our present want of a Minister may be no way imputed to our Negligence, think it not amiss to acquaint Yr Excellency our utmost Sedulity hath not been wanting to procure one, and hope the little chance in this country will, in some sort, excuse our delay, together with ye refusal of one whom we desired to entertain. We shall also use our Sincere Endeavours to supply ye Vacancy, and give due obedience to Law. We are, with all submission, Yr Excellency's most humble and obedient servants,

Signed by all ye Vestry."

"On the 12th June, 1704, the Churchwardens were empowered to procure a Minister, and the subjoined declaration was also put upon record:

"Whereas Mr. Solomon Whateley hath of late preached in this Parish (which for some time before he had forebore to do,) this Vestry do declare that he doth it not any way with their consent or approbation, and that they think themselves no way obliged to pay him for ye same." Mr. Whateley delivered, on the same day, into the hands of Philip Ludwell, Churchwarden, the sum of ten pound, charity money, which was in his hands; and before adjournment the following was recorded:

"June ye twelfth, 1704,
Entered by Command of His Excellency,
Coll: Phil. Ludwell, } CWs. Mr. John Page,
Mr. William Pinkethman,   Mr. Wm. Timson,
Mr. Henry Tyler,   Mr. Wm. Hansford.
Capt. Hugh Norwell,

"As to ye Number of Vestrymen that Mett ye 22 day of May last, there were six beside Yr Minister, which his Excellency Ye Governour declares to be a Vestry, being six, the Major part of eleaven; & Coll. Ludwell affirmed that six was not ye Major part,—but to make no dispute ye Minister being present.

"The Vestry's answer to Sir Edward Northy's Opinion, and ye order of Council being read out of ye Book, his Excellency was pleased to Command all ye Gentlemen of ye Vestry to attend him att the Royal College of William and Mary on Monday, ye nineteenth of this Instant, about ten o'clock. Her Majesty's Attorney General, Mr. Wharton, and Mr. Holloway being gone to ye County Court."

On the 19th day of February, 1705,

"Whereas there was an Information Exhibited by ye last General Court by the Attorney General in behalf of her Majesty against ye Vestry of this Parish, and writs thereupon being issued, Commanding ye appearance of ye Vestrymen therein named to Answer ye said information ye Next General Court, the Vestry doe think fitt to desire & Impower Coll. Philip Ludwell and Mr. Wm. Pinkethman, ye present Churchwardens, ... to defend and manage ye said suit."

"The following will show that while there was a disposition on the part of Governor Nicholson to conciliate the Vestry, yet the course pursued by that worthy functionary, in regard to the forcing upon them the Rev. Mr. Whateley, had not been forgotten on their parts; and though they accept the gift of "his Excellency," it is done with such a sly insinuation that one cannot help thinking they understood him and his motives better than he suspected.

Induction Controversy

"At a Vestry held for Bruton Parish ye 7th August, 1705,"
.... "His Excellency the Governour sending to this Vestry (by ye hand of Mr. Wm. Robertson) An Altar Cloth and Cushion as a present for ye use of ye Parish, together with fifty shillings for ye use of ye poor, and desiring ye said gift of fifty shillings might be recorded in the Vestry book as being his Excellency's usuall quarterly gift; and also what his Excellency hath formerly given, together with an account how ye same hath been disposed of,—The Vestry return this answer by Mr. Robertson, (viz.) We return his Excellency many thanks for ye Altar Cloth, and also for ye fifty shillings now sent—which we assure his Excellency's shall be registered; but not knowing it to be his Excellency's Constant Custom, we cannot register it as such without we know att present what his Excellency hath given to the poor; but we do promise to examine that matter against ye next Vestry, and what appears to us, then shall be registered."

Patience, perseverance, and, doubtless, prudence on the part of Mr. Whateley, together with a show of right in his favor, and gubernatorial countenance, at last wrought a change in the minds of the Vestry, and accordingly like those who felt it was "good and pleasant for brethren to dwell together in unity," on the 25th October, 1705, the Vestry made the following order, reserving however those "inalienable rights" which subsequent years incorporated in the great Declaration of American Independence.

"At a Vestry held for Bruton Parish ye 25th October, 1705, Present—

Phil. Ludwell, Esq.
Mr. Wm. Pinkethman, } CWs
Edmunds Jennings, Esq.
Captain Hugh Norwell,

Mr. John Page,
Capt. Wm. Timson,
Mr. Wm. Hansford,
Mr. ffred: Jones,

"The Vestry taking into consideration that Mr. Solomon Whateley hath been serviceable to ye parish in reading Divine Service, and also in Preaching severall Sermons, from ye first of May, 1704, to this time, and though he did not officiate by ye direction or approbation of ye Vestry, Yet it being thought fitt yt he should have some satisfaction for his trouble,—the Vestry hath agreed to give ye said Mr. Whateley Sixteen thousand pounds of Tobacco and Caske, as a gratuity for all past service to this time,—and the Vestry have thought fitt to propose to ye said Mr. Whateley to Officiate as Minister of this Parish from this time to ye first of May Next, provided Nevertheless that any thing herein contained shall not be construed as the Vestry's owning Mr. Whateley to be Minister of this Parish for ye time past. Mr. Whateley agreed."

"Att a Vestry held ye fifth day of December, 1706, Mr. Solomon Whateley, Mr. Wm. Hansford, and Mr. Joseph White, having desired to take ye oath appointed to be taken instead of ye oaths of Allegiance and Supremacy, The President of Her Majesty's Council did this day administer the same, and they subscribed the Test."

The period had arrived when Mr. Whateley was called to "go the way of all flesh," and it must have gladdened the heart of the old grey-haired Minister, that although at his election in 1705, it was specified he should be employed only until the next May, he was permitted to remain in uninterrupted occupancy until "death did them part."* The last Vestry he attended was held the 14th September, 1710, and at a Vestry held 20th November, 1710, his decease is announced.

"Mr. John Page having acquainted the Vestry that he hath removed out of this Parish, & desiring ye Vestry to appoint Another in his room, they have thought fitt to make choice of Mr. David Bray, &c."†

---

* For more of Mr. Whateley and "other clergy" who figured in the Colony at and about this time, see Dr. Hawks' "Colonial Church Papers," in Church Review for 1851.

† Both of these gentlemen were distinguished in their day and generation. The first named held prominent office, (was subsequently Governor,) and retiring from active public life, married Mary Mann, an heiress of Gloucester, and built "Rosewell," the famed seat of elegance and hospitality for more than a century. Mr. Bray filled several offices of trust and honor.

THE CHURCH YARD.

Appendix B

Epitaphs and Inscriptions on Mural Tablets and Tombstones in Bruton Parish Church and Church Yard from 1678 to 1800

THE following inscriptions from the mural tablets in Bruton Church, and from the tomb-stones in Bruton Church yard, from 1678 to 1800, were published in Vol. XI, of Virginia Historical Society collections in 1891, by Professor J. L. Hall, Ph. D., of William and Mary College. The foot notes appended were inserted by Mr. R. A. Brock, the Corresponding Secretary and Librarian of the Society. We are glad, by the kind permission of these gentlemen, to make use of this material, for, as Dr. Hall remarks, "the hand of time, and of the vandal, more remorseless than time, is fast chipping away our sepulchral marbles." Some of the inscription copied then could not now be taken from the tombs with the same degree of accuracy. To these inscriptions published in 1891 a few others of special interest, though of later date, have been added.

It is unfortunate that an "Association for the Preservation of Virginia Antiquities" was not formed long years ago. By the thoughtful and loving care of the Society now in existence, what remains of the ancient past is being carefully guarded and preserved; but many monuments of the olden days were destroyed before interest in their preservation was aroused. There are persons, now living in Williamsburg, who remember when there were many monuments in Bruton Church-yard which now no longer remain.

Tablets in Bruton Church

The Parke Mural Tablet

Near this Marble Lyes
ye Honble Daniel Parke
of ye County of Essex Esq who
was one of his Ma:^{ties} Counsellers
and some time Secretary of the
Collony of Virg:^a he Died ye 6th of
March Anno 1679
His other felicityes ware Crowned by
his happy Marridg with Rebbecka
the daughter of George Evelyn
of the County of Surry Esq she dyed
the 2^d of Ianuary Anno 1672 at Long
Ditton in ye County of Surry and
left behind her a most
hopefull progeny[1]

The Orlando Jones Tablet, in Aisle

Here lies in hope of a Blessed Resurrection
the Body of Mr Orlando Iones Son of M
Rowland Iones, some time Minister of
this Parish. he was born December ye 31st 1681
and Died Iune ye 12th 1719 in ye 38th year of his
Age. he was twice Married his first Wife wa[s]

---

[1] Colonel Daniel Parke had issue: two daughters—Francis, who married John Custis; and Lucy, the first wife of Colonel William Byrd of "Westover," the second of the name. Colonel Parke went to England, where he was appointed an aid-de-camp to the Duke of Marlborough; was with him at the battle of Blenheim, and was selected to convey the news of that memorable victory to Queen Anne. He was subsequently appointed Governor of the Leward Islands, and was slain in an insurrection there.—R. A. BROCK.

Mrs Martha Macon² Daughter of Mr Gideon
Macon of New-Kent by whom he left one
Son Named Lane & one Daughter Named
Frances, his Second Wife was Mrs Mary
Williams, Daughter of Iames Williams
of King & Queen County, who Erected this
Monument to his Memory.

The Cocke Mural Tablet

MDLCCLII
Inscribed to the Memory of
Dr. William Cocke,
An English Physician, Born of reputable Parents
MDCLXXII
at Sudbury in Suffolk,
and Educated at Queen's College, Cambridge,
He was learned and polite,
of indisputed Skill in his profession,
of unbounded Generosity in his practice:
which multitudes, yet alive, can testify.
He was, many years, of the Council
and Secretary of State, for this Colony
In the Reign of Queen Anne & of King George
He died Suddenly, sitting a Judge upon the Bench
of the General Court in the Capitol:
MDCCXX
His Hon: friend Alexa Spotswood, Esqr then Govr

---

²⁸ She was married January 31, 1703; died May 11, 1716, and is buried at the Macon homestead in New Kent county. Her daughter Frances is said to have been the wife of Colonel John Dandridge and the mother of Martha (Dandridge-Custis) Washington. Gideon Macon, by tradition, was at one time the Secretary of Sir William Berkeley. He was for a time an Indian interpreter. The Christian name of his wife was Martha. Colonel John Dandridge died in 1756, aged fifty-six years. His tomb is in St. George's church-yard, Fredericksburg, Virginia.—
R. A. Brock.

with the principal Gentlemen of the Country,
attended his funeral,
and, weeping, saw the Corps Interred
at the West side of the Alter,
in this Church.[3]

The Tyler Mural Tablet

In Memoriam.
HENRY TYLER, SR. & HENRY TYLER, JR.
Vestrymen & Wardens of Bruton
Church & Parish.
John Tyler & Elizabeth Low, parents of
Joanna Tyler-McKenzie & John Tyler
the Marshall of the Colony of Va.:
& Anne Contesse, parents of
John Tyler,
Patriot, Gov'r, Judge of the Admiralty,
Supreme & U. S. Courts of Va.:
& Mary Armistead,
of Buck-Rowe, parents of
John Tyler,
Student, Visitor, Rector & Chancellor
of Wm. & Mary College:
Gov'r, Member of Congress, Senator,
Vice President and President of the United
States, Member of Confederate Congress:
& Laetitia Christian, parents of
Robert Tyler, Poet, Philosopher, States-
man, Gentleman, Samuel Tyler, A. B., LL. D.
Chancellor of the State of Va.,

---

3 Dr. Cocke married Elizabeth, sister of Mark Catesby, the natural-
ist, and had issue, whose descendants include the names of Archer, Battaile, Buckner, Dudley, Gregory, Hansford, Holliday, Jones, Laughlin,
Montgomery, Taliaferro, Taylor, Washington and others. His widow
married secondly Colonel John Holloway, an eminent lawyer of Williamsburg, Virginia. She died March 4, 1755, aged 74 years.—R. A. BROCK.

Grandson of the Marshall.
This tablet is erected by some
of their Descendants:
June 1888, A. D.

Governor Francis Fauquier

Under the church, doubtless, were buried many to whom no stone was erected. Governor Fauquier was buried under the north wing of the church, but no monument to him remains. His death and obsequies are described in the Virginia Gazette of March 3, 1768, as follows:

"Early this morning, died at the palace, after a tedious illness, which he bore with the greatest patience and fortitude, the Hon. Francis Fauquier, Esq., Lieutenant-Governor and Commander-in-Chief of the Colony, over which he has presided near ten years, much to his own honor, and the ease and satisfaction of the inhabitants. He was a gentleman of the most amiable disposition, generous, just and mild, and possessed, in an eminent degree, of all the social virtues. He was a fellow of the Royal Society, and died in his 65th year."

The Wilmer Mural Tablet

In
Memory
of
the Rev'd. William H. Wilmer, D. D.,
whose eminent talents and exemplary Piety
enabled him to fill with dignity
the important stations of
Rector of this Church
President of Wm. & Mary College
President of the House of Clerical

and Lay Deputies of the Protestant
Episcopal Church.
He was beloved in Private
Respected and honored in Public Life
A Sound Devine
A Faithful Pastor
A sincere and Practical Christian
Born in Chester-Town, Maryland,
March 9th, 1784
Died July 24th, 1827

This Monument is erected by the Congregation
and Christians of other denominations
in testimony of their profound respect
and ardent affection
for the deceased.

Confederate Soldiers Memorial Mural Tablet

On the wall of the Church, near the south-east corner where the old pulpit stood, is a marble tablet to the memory of the Confederate soldiers who fell in the battle of Williamsburg. It is inscribed:

In memory of
the
Confederate
Soldiers
who fell in the
Battle of Williamsburg
May the 5th, 1862
And of those who died of
the wounds received in
the same.

They died for us.

Tomb-stone Inscriptions

John Yuille

Here Lyes the Corps of John
Yuille Merchant Son to Thomas
Yuile of Darleith in the County of
D .... on Scotland who died at
W ..... burgh in Virginia upon
the 2 .... day of October 1746 years
in the 27th year of his Age.

Numine et Virtute
[Arms] 4

John Collett

Here lyes the Body of
Mr John Collett
who departed this Life
February 24th 1749, Aged 52 Years

Hugh Orr

Here lyes the corps
of Hugh Orr hammer
man in Williamsburg
who died Jan'ry 6th 1764
aged 54 years.

---

4 Burke, "General Armory," gives as arms of Yuille, (London), and Yule, (Darleith, Scotland): Ar. on a fesse betw. three crescents sa. a garb or, branded gu.

Crest,—An ear of wheat ppr. leaved vert.

Motto. Numine et virtute.

No criticism is intended in the remark that Professor Hall does not describe verbally or pictorially arms appearing with the inscriptions. As he does not, however, the editor can be guided in annotation only by such information as he possesses and by apprehension. In the daily increasing regard for family history, coat-armor is an important guide in linking families with remote ancestry.

Ann Charlton

Here lies y^e
Body of ANN
CHARLTON
wife of George
Charlton who
Died Sep
in the
Year of her
Age.

Robert Rae

R [Arms] R
Here Lies the Body
of Robert Rae Mer
hant in Falmouth
son of Robert Rae
Esqr of Little Govan
near Glasgow in
North Britain, he
departed this Life
May 30 1753
in the 30 year of his
Age.

Mary Nicolson

Here lies
the body of
Mary Nicolson
the wife of Robert Nicolson,

who departed this life
Oct. 10th 1793,[5]
In the 73d year of her age.

Mrs. Ann Burges

Here sleeps in Jesus united to Him
by faith and the Graces of a Christian
life, all that was Mortal of Mrs. Ann Burges
once the tender and affectionate Wife
of the Revd Henry John Burges,
of the Isle of Wight: She died 25th
December 1771 in giving Birth to an
Infant Daughter, who rests in her Arms.
She here waits the transporting Moment
when the Trump of God shall call her
forth to Glory. Honour & Immortality,
Oh DEATH where is thy Sting?
Oh GRAVE where is thy Victory?

Ann Frank

Here Lyeth the Body of Ann
the Wife of Graham Frank[6]
and Daughter of the Revd Mr
Theods Staige who died on
the feast of St Andrew 1759
Aged 28 years[7]

---

[5] These were, it is believed, the parents of two worthy sons: Robert, a surgeon in the army of the Revolution, and George Nicolson, who was Mayor of Richmond in 1790, and subsequently. One of the daughters of the latter was the wife of the late Rev. George Woodbridge, D. D., so long the beloved rector of the Monumental (Episcopal) church.—R. A. BROCK.

[6] Bishop Meade ("Old Churches and Families of Virginia," Vol. I, p. 203) mentions Graham Frank as a merchant of London, and a correspondent of Rev. Samuel Shield and of the Nelsons.

[7] Rev. Theodosius Staige came, with an unmarried sister, to Virginia, and was the rector of St. George's parish, Spotsylvania county, some time prior to November, 1728. He served also for a time York-Hampton parish. Another sister (Letitia Maria Ann) had married in

Mary Purdie

Here Lyes Interred the
Remains of Mary Purdie Wife of
Alex^r Purdie Printer who departed
This Life On Saturday ye 28, of March
1772 in the 27 year of her age. She left
Behind her four sons Ja^s Hugh Alex^r
and William, and by her side lie Jane
a dear little Daughter who did not
quite attain her second year. She
was a virtuous loving, frugal and
discreet wife, an affectionate, though
discerning Mother, one of the best
of Mistresses. As friend and Ac
quaintance, she possessed the Qua
lifications which render that Con
nection valuable for she was Sen
sible Prudent Generous and
honest hearted no deceit lay un
der her Tongue. Her husband
in Gratitude for the ardent affection
she bore him the genuine esteem he
had for her and in Justice to her
Virtues caused this stone to be
placed over her It will on
day serve to con[8]

London Rev. James Marye, a native of Rouen, Normandy, France, the ancestor of the well-known Virginia family of the name. (See Descendants of, in "Huguenot Emigration to Virginia," *Virginia Historical Collections*, Vol. V.) Another daughter of Mr. Staige married Samuel Thompson, Orange county, Virginia, and they had issue, among others possibly, a son, William Staige. The name Staige is a favored Christian name in the Davis and other families of Virginia. A distinguished instance was the late Prof. John Staige Davis, M D., of the University of Virginia.—R. A. BROCK.

[8] Alexander Purdie was for years public printer of the colony, and the publisher in his own name and as a member of the firm of Purdie & [John] Dixon, of *The Virginia Gazette*.—R. A. BROCK.

Buckner Stith

Here lyes the Bodies of [BUCK]
NER STITH [9] and CATHERINE STITH
Son and Eldest Daughter of
Stith of Northampton County.
Buckner a hopeful Youth
[born] the 3d Day of January 1747 [departed]
the Life in this City the
of December 1766.

*   *   *   *   *

died an Infant Eighteen days old

Also the Body of
Mrs Catherine Blackley late of this City
Grandmother of the above Named Children
She departed this Life the 25th Day of
October 1771 Aged 73 Years and upwards.

James Grinley

Memento Mori
Here lyeth the Corps
of James Grinley
son of Alexr Grinley
in Dunbar Scotland
Who Departed
this life the 10 Day
of Jully 1763
in the Twentyeth
year of his Age.

---

[9] The children of Griffin and Mary (Blackley) Stith. Griffin Stith was a son of Drury and Susannah (Bathurst) Stith, nephew of Rev. Mr. Stith, the historian, and grandson of Colonel John Stith, who patented land in Charles City county in 1663, and was High Sheriff in 1691.—R. A. BROCK.

Joseph Scrivener

Here lieth the Body of M^r· Joseph
Scrivener who was born at Oldney
in Buckinghamshire in England
and died here the 14th of October
1772 in the fiftieth Year of His Age.

Michael Archer

Here Lies ye Body
of Michael Archer Gent^t
who was Born ye 29 of Sept^r.
1681 Near Rippon in Yorkshire
And died ye 10 of February 1726
in ye 46 year of his Age.

Also Joanna Archer
Wife of Michael Archer who
Departed this life
Octo^r 1, 1732[10]

Judith Greenhow

In memory of Judith Greenhow
a sincere Christian
She died the Seventh day
of January 1765
and in the 29 year of her age

---

[10] Michael Archer was clerk of James City county from 1719, and perhaps earlier, until his death. George Archer, believed to be the ancestor of the Archers of Henrico, Amelia, Powhatan and other counties, patented 550 acres of land in Henrico county, June 2, 1665 (Book V, p. 69, Land Registry.)

How loved how valued once avails thee not[11]
To whom Related or by whom begot!
A heap of Dust alone remains of thee,
So all thou art, and all the proud shall be

Thomas Hornsby

Here lies in hopes of a Blessed
Resurrection, the Remains
of Mr Thomas Hornsby
who was for many Years
a Merchant in this City.
He was Born in Lincolnshire
in England,
January 17th 1702
and died May 27th 1772
the Remains
of Mrs Margaret Hornsby
Wife of Mr Thomas Hornsby
who died February 2 1770
Aged 66 years.[12]

From a book-plate of William Archer, a descendant, which has been preserved, the family appears to have been from Cornwall, England.

Frederick Johnston, in his meritorious "Memorials of Virginia Clerks," laments the destruction of the records of James City county, in the burning of the court-house in Richmond, April 3, 1865, and commences his list of clerks of the county with Leonard A. Henley, 1831.—R. A. BROCK.

[11] Somewhat mutilated; but I have completed the lines by reference to Pope.

[12] Thomas Hornsby was highly esteemed and very successful as a merchant. Joseph Hornsby, probably his son, was a vestryman of Bruton parish in 1774.—R. A. BROCK.

Edward Nott

[Arms]
Under this Marble Rests ye Ashes
of His Excellency Edward Nott
Late Governor of this Collony who
In his Private character was a good
Christian and in his Public a good
Governor he was A lover of Mankind
And Bountiful to his friends By ye
Sanctity of his Moralls and ye Mildness
Prudence and justice of his Administra-
tion he was Deservedly Esteemed A
Public Blessing while he Lived & when
He Dyed A Public Callamity. he Departed
This Life the 23d Day of August 1706
Aged 49 Years.
In Gratefull Remembrance of who
se many Dutyes the Generall Assembly
of this Collony have Erected this
Monument.[13]

James Nicolson

Sacred
to the memory of
James Nicolson
late steward of
William and Marys College
he was born in the town of Inverners

---

[13] Edward Nott entered upon his duties as Lieutenant-Governor August 15, 1705. He procured the passage by the Assembly of an act for the building of a "palace" for the Governor, with an appropriation of £3,000, also an act establishing the general court; but the last was disallowed by the British Board of Trade. During Governor Nott's administration the College of William and Mary was destroyed by fire.— R. A. BROCK.

NORTH-BRITAIN
ANNO 1711
and died the 22d of January
1773
industry. frugality. integrity.
simplicity. of manners and
independence of SOUL
Adorned his Character and
procured him Universal Esteem
READER
Learn from this Example that
As the most Exalted station may
be debased by VICE so there
is no situation in life on
which VIRTUE will not confer
DIGNITY!

Charles Hunt

To the Memory of
Mr Charles Hunt
late of this Parish.
He died the 11th day
of Octr 1794
Aged 41 Years.
Regretted by all who knew him.

Katherine Thorp

Katherine Thorp
Relick of Capt Thomas
Thorp Nephew to Major
Otho Thorp formerly
Inhabitant of this Parish
after a Pilgrimage of forty

three yeares in a Troublesome
world Lay Downe here to
Rest in hope of a Joyfull
Resurection obiit June 6th
1695

Thomas Thorp

Here lyeth in Hope of a joyfull
Resurrection the Body of Capt
Thomas Thorp of Bruton
Parish in the Dominion of Virginia
Nephew of Maj. Otho Thorp
of the same Parish who Departed
This Life the 7 day of October
Ano 1693 Aged 48

Edwardus Barradall

[Arms] [14]
H S E
EDWARDUS BARRADALL Armiger
Qui
In legum studiis feliciter versatus
Attornati Generalis et Admiralitatis Iudicis
Amplicissimus Partes merito obtinuit
fideliter obivit

---

[14] From a rough drawing in the possession of the editor, the arms of Barradall (tinctures not given), a bend, three pheons, an annulet for difference, are impaled with Fitzhugh—Az.: three chevrons bracedin base of escutcheon, or, a chief of the last. William Fitzhugh, lawyer, planter, merchant and shipper, the ancestor of the well-known family of the name, was born in Bedford, England, January 9, 1651; settled in that portion of Stafford, now comprising Prince George county; died at his seat, Bedford, Virginia, in October, 1701.—R. A. BROCK.

Collegium Gulielmi et Mariæ
Cum Gubernator
Tum in Conventu Generali Senator
Propugnavit
SARAM
Viri Honorabilis
Guil Fitzhugh Armigeri
Serenissimae Reginae Annæ in Virginia a Consilios
Filiam Natu minimam
Tam Mortis quam Vitae Sociam
Uxorem habuit.
Obierunt

ille XIII Cal Iulii A D. MDCCXLIII Æ { XXXIX
illa   Non Oct   { XXX

Hic iuxta situs est
Henricus Barradall
E. B. supra dicti frater
Qui
Obiit XVIII Cal Octob A. D. MDCCXXXVII
Ætat XXVII
Blumfield Barradall tantum frater[15]

The epitaph of *Rev. Roland Jones*, first rector of Bruton Parish. Bishop Meade is not accurate. Owing to the ignorance of workmen recently employed in the churchyard, the epitaph is permanently distorted. The following is approximately correct:

Revd. Rolandus Iones

Hic jacet Rolandus Iones
clericus filius Rolandi Jones
clerici Natus Swimbrook juxta
Burford in Comii Oxoii Collegii
Merton Universitate Oxoii

---

[15] Last few lines so badly worn as to be illegible.

Alumnus Parochiae Bruton Virginia
Pastor Primus & delectissimus
funenone Pastorali annis 14
fideliter d   Parochiae quam
maximo de   Obiit Ap 23
die Ætatis suae 48 Anno D 1688

Margaret Brown

Here Lyes the Body of
Margaret Brown wife to
Doctor John Brown of Williamsburg
late of Cold Stream North Britain
who died the 22^d day of August 1720
in the 36 year of Her Age
Prob! Dolor quao fuit Clarissime.

Here Lyes the Body of Jane Brown
Daughter to the foresaid John Brown
who died the 30 August 1720 the
14 day of Her Age.

Thomas Ludwell

[Arms] [16]
Under this Marble lieth the Body
of Thomas Ludwell Esqr
Secretary of Virginia, who was born
at Bruton in the County of Somerset
in the Kingdom of ENGLAND, and
departed this Life in the Year 1678 And
near this place lye the Bodies of Richard

---

[16] The arms upon the book-plate of Philip Ludwell of "Green Spring" are: Gu, a bend ar., three eagles displayed sa. between three towers. *Motto*—Pensieri stretti edil viso sciolto.—R. A. BROCK.

Kemp, Esqr his Predecessor in ye Secretarys Office[17] and Sr Thomas Lunsford Kt in Memory of whom this Marble is placed by Order of Philip Ludwell Esqr Nephew of the said Thomas Ludwell in the Year 1727

Iohn Greenhow

Here lies
in hopes of a joyful
Resurrection all that was
mortal of Iohn Greenhow,
late of this City, Merchant,
He was born in Staunton,
near Kendal in Westmoreland,
Great Britain, November the 12th
1724 & died the 29th August 1787,
after a very short Illness.
On his left side lies Elizabeth

---

[17] Richard Kemp was a member of the Council of Virginia, 1642, and as its President in June, 1644, upon the departure of Sir William Berkeley for England, became the acting Governor of the Colony. It is notable that during his incumbency the first fast and thanksgiving days in the Colony, of which any record is preserved, were ordered. "Att James Cittye the 17th of February, 1644-5," it was "enacted by the Governour, Counsell and Burgesses of this present Grand Assembly, for God's glory and the publick benefit of the Collony to the end that God might avert his heavie judgments that are now upon vs, That the last Wednesday in every month be sett apart for a day of ffast and humiliation. And that it be wholly dedicated to prayers and preaching." Also, "That the eighteenth day of April be yearly celebrated by thanksgivings for our deliverance from the hands of Salvages." Referring to the recent massacre by the Indians (*Hening's Statutes*, I, pp. 289, 290.) Sir William Berkeley returning in June, 1645, resumed the government of Virginia, but Richard Kemp continued to serve the Colony as a member of the Council until 1648, and perhaps later, latterly as the Secretary of the body. He died some time before 1678—R. A. BROCK.

the Daughter of Iohn Tyler[18]
his second Wife,
who was born in James City
the 30th Jany 1744, and died
of the Small Pox on July the 23rd 1781
which she endured with the greatest
Christian fortitude & Resignation.

Edward Dyer

Here Lyeth
Edward Dyer
Who died Octr
ye 6 1722 agd
1 Year & 7 Mo
ye Only Son of
Rob Dyer &
Martha his
Wife

Jean Blair

In the adjoining grave lies deposited
with her husband whatever was mortal of
Jean Blair,
who was born 26th Octr 1736, O. S.
and died 22nd Novr 1792
Her conduct through life was truly exemplary and
amiable in discharging all the relative duties of her
station as a wife, a mother and a friend; and her piety
shone forth with peculiar lustre during a protracted,
painful, and distressing illness, which she sustained

---

[18] Marshal of the Colony and grandfather of President John Tyler.
—R. A. Brock.

without a murmur, with entire resignation and
acknowledgments of the divine mercy and goodness;
and fervent prayers to be released, and, resign her
spirit to God Who gave it.
Here lies interred
the body of James Blair
son of the Honble John Blair [19]
a youth distinguished for the uniform purity
of his morals, accompanied with ingenuous modesty
and the most winning mildness of temper and manners.
He was born the 9th of June 1770
and died the 25th of Octr 1791.

Jane Blair

SACRED to the memory of
JANE, the youngest daughter of
the Honble John Blair,
and beloved wife of James Henderson [20]
Mournful and with tears, he hath erected
this last gift of love and conjugal affection.
She died 19th Decr 1800
Aged 40 years.
Having been distinguished for her piety
affection, prudence, and suavity of manners.
At her feet are deposited the bodies

---

[19] John Blair, son of Dr. Archibald Blair, and nephew of Rev. James Blair, D. D., President of William and Mary College; member of the House of Burgesses in 1736; long a member of the Council, of which as President, he was acting Governor of Virginia for a time in 1758. His son, Archibald Blair, was Secretary of the Virginia Convention of 1776; and another son, John Blair, a Justice of the Supreme Court of the United States. A daughter, Jane, was the first wife of James Henderson.—R. A. BROCK.

[20] James Henderson married secondly——, and had issue; 1. James; 2. Walter; 3. Elizabeth. He died in 1818, and William Brown and Alexander Brown were his executors.—R. A. BROCK.

of her three infant children,
James Blair, born 29th Oct 1795,
and lived only 21 days.
John Blair, born 25th Feby 1797
and died 17th April following, and
Blair Monroe, born 30th July, 1800
and died 4th May 1801.

David Bray

[Arms][21]
Here Lyeth the Body of
COLONEL David Bray
of this Parish
who died on ye 21 of Octr 1717
in the 52^d Year of His Age
and Left
his Wife Judith & Son David Bray
by whom this Monument was Erected
in Memory of Him
Under this tomb with her husband
Lieth Mrs Judith Bray who
Departed this Life the 26 Day
of October MDCCXX in the
45th Year of her Age.[22]

---

[21] Az. a chevron between three eagles' legs erased a la cuisse sa. armed gu. *Crest*—An ounce ppr.—R. A. BROCK.

[22] James [1] Bray was the first of the name in Virginia of whom record is preserved. He was living in James City county in 1666, was sworn a member of the Council March 4, 1674–'5; married Angelica ———, and had issue: 1. Thomas;[2] 2. James,[2] J. P. of James City county, 1710, and later; vestryman of Bruton parish; sheriff, 1717–'18; married in or before 1698 Mourning, widow of Colonel Thomas Pettus. He had (with, perhaps other issue) a son, Thomas,[3] J. P. of James City county, 1738, who had an only child, Elizabeth,[4] who married Colonel Philip Johnson, of King & Queen county, and died in 1675. 3. Colone David,[2] *supra* vestryman of Bruton Parish, and J. P. of James City

James Bray

[Arms]
Here Lyeth in . .
of Iames Br . .
as Bray by whom
this Monument was Erected

James   Bray
1690

Another *Bray* monument—marble pyramidal shaft on a marble die, the latter having handsome armorial bearings on two sides and Latin inscriptions on the other two.[23]

David Bray

H. S. E.
David Bray Armiger
Vir
Forma Ingenio Morum Suavitate et Comitate Praetor
Serenissimo Regi Georgio Secundo
Conciliis in Virginia constitubus
Tamen ante Munus Susceptum florente Ætate
Morte abreptus.
Elisabetham
Iohannis Page, Arminger[24] Filiam Natu primam

---

county, 1710. He had issue: 1. David, 3 *infra*, born 1699; member of the council; died 1731; married Elizabeth, daughter of John Page of Gloucester county. 4. Angelica, married Mungo Inglis of Williamsburg the first Master of the Grammar School, William and Mary College (1693-1719.) His descendants intermarried with the Armisteads, Pages and Sheildses.

The widow of Thomas Bray established a scholarship at William and Mary College.—R. A. BROCK.

[23] The arms of Bray with an inescutcheon bearing the Page arms.
—R. A. BROCK.

[24] Errors in cutting.

Sibi Matrimonio conjunctam habuit
Mutuo Affectus conjunctissimam.
et sine Prote maerentem reliquit
Octob 5º 1731 Ætat 32
Illa Amoris Conjugalii Extremum Pignus
Hoc Monumentum posuit

Elizabetha Bray

Hic Depositum
Quicquid habuit Mortale Elizabetha Bray
Una cum Marito desideratissimo.
Quae languenti morbo consumpta Animam
Resignavit 22º Die Aprilis Anno 1734
Ætatis 32º
Æquanimiter, fortiter, Pie.

James Whaley

Here lieth the Body of James Whaley
of Yorke County in Virginia who
departed this life the 16 day of May
Anno Domini 1701 and in the fiftieth
yeare of his Age
His Body lyes to be Consumed to Dust
Till the Resurrection of the Just
Amongst Which Number He'll in hopes Appeare
His blessed Sentence at doomsday to heare

Mathew Whaley

[25] Mathew Whaley lyes Interred here
Within this Tomb upon his father dear.
Who Departed

---

[25] Square piece of marble on the front face of the monument.

this Life the 26th of
September 1705 Aged
Nine years only child
of Iames Whaley
and Mary his wife

Fragment of *Colonel John Page's* tombstone, lying near the west door of Bruton Parish church, within the building.

Iohn Page

[Arms]²⁶

Here lieth in hope of a Joyfull Resurrection
the Body of Colonel Iohn Page of
Bruton Parish Esquire one of their
Majesties Council in the Dominion
[of] Virginia w o Departed this
[life t]he 23 of [Ja]nuary in the year
[of our] Lord 69½ Aged 65

Alice Page

Wife of Colonel John Page

[Arms]²⁷

Here lyeth the Body of Alice Page
wife to Iohn Page of ye county of York
in Virginia   aged 73 yeares who
departed this life the 22 day of june
Anno Domini 1698

---

²⁶ Arms: Ar., a fesse dancette between three martlets; azure, a bordure of the last. *Crest:* A demi-horse forcene (rearing).—R. A. BROCK.

²⁷ Colonel John Page married, about 1656, Alice Luckin, of county Essex, England. In the "Page Family of Virginia," by Dr. R. C. M. Page, New York, 1883, it is stated (p. 41) that the arms on this tomb were those of Luckin: Sable, a fesse indented between two leopard's faces or. *Crest*—A demi-griffin or., issuing out of a tower paly of six of the last and sable.—R. A. BROCK.

Francis Page

[Arms]

Here lieth in hope of a Joyfull Resurrection
the Body of Captain Francis Page of
Bruton Parish in the Dominion of Virginia
Eldest Son of Colonel Iohn Page of the
Same Parish, Esquire, Who Departed
this life the tenth Day of May
in the Year of our Lord
1692: Aged 35
Thou wast while living of Unspotted fame
Now being Dead, no man Dares Soil thy name
for thou wast One whom Nothing here Could Stain
ither force of honour nor Love of Gain
spheres thou hast well Discharg'd thy trust
most truly Pious, Loyal Iust
stant Goodness my Penn Cannt Express
Vertues my tongue Cannt Rehearse
steem'd by all the wise and Sage
thy country in thy age
we Cannt Now Speak of the
eet to all Posterity
Did to Yoursef Create
erlasting Date
your most happy wife
other Life

Mary Page

[Arms][28]

Here lieth in the hope of a Joyfull Resurrection
the body of Mary, the wife of Captain
Francis Page of Bruton Parish in
the Dominion of Virginia, Daughter of

---

[28] The editor has no information as to these arms, whether of Page alone or impaled with those of Digges. The latter are: Gu. on a cross ar., five eagles displayed sa. armed of the field.—R. A. BROCK.

Edward Diggs of Hampton Parish in
the Same Dominion, Esquire who Departed
this life the Eighteenth Day of March in
the year of Our Lord 169°, Aged 3[2?]
Thy Modest, meek and Pious Soule did Shine
With well-Tempered Nature and Grace Divine
One to Excell in beauty few Could Finde
yet thy Rarest features were of the minde
thou wast a faithful and Vertuous wife
thou Greatly Loved peace and hated strife
thou wast a prudent and tender Mother
a true-loving sister to Each Brother
a Choice friend a Kind Nighbour
a good Christian ready at God's call
thou lived and dy'd upon Christ Relying
thou Dy'd to Sin and now Livest by Dying
thy faith Doth yield thy Piety Doth Give
Restoratives to make thee Ever live
thrice blest friend this Epitaph is thy due
when Saints arise thy Lord will say 'tis true.

Elizabeth Page

[Arms]

Here lyeth the body of Elizabeth Page, dec^d
late wife to Iohn Page of Yorke [co]unty Gent.
and Daughter of [C]ap^t Francis Page late of the
same County deceased she blest her sa[id]
Husband w[ith] A Somm and Daughter & departed
this life the 12 day of November Anno Dom 1702
And in the 20 yeare of her age.

Mrs. Ann Timson Jones

Here lies all that the grave can claim of
Mrs. Ann Timson Jones
Consort of the

Rev. Servant Jones
Born 1st Sept. 1787
Married 26 Dec. 1805
Baptised 3 Mar. 1822
Died June 6, 1849.

If woman ever yet did well
If woman ever did excell
If woman husband ere adored
If woman ever loved the Lord
If ever faith and Hope and Love
In Human flesh did live and move
If all the graces ere did meet
In her in her they were complete

My Ann, my all my Angel Wife
My dearest one my love my life
I cannot sigh or say fare well
But where thou dwellest I will dwell.

In Memory of the Confederate Soldiers

In the church-yard is a monument to their memory which bears the following inscription:

Lord keep their memory green.

Erected to the memory of the Confederate Soldiers who fell in the Battle of Williamsburg, May 5th, 1862, and lie buried under and around this monument.

R. Crawford,	14th Louisiana Inf.	
J. M. Cary,	" "	"
Wm. Baldridge, 18th Mississippi		"
John Daisy, 8th Reg., Alabama		"
D. Dargan, "	"	"
T. D. Darr, 10th Reg.	"	"
T. H. More, " "	"	"
D. H. Woolley " "	"	"

C. M. Blackburn, 10th Reg., Alabama Inf.
P. R. Wright, 13th Reg., Nth. Car. "
W. D. Mooney, " " " " "
James Barnett, 19th Reg., Virginia "
James Keating, 17th " " "
W. L. Rector, 11th " " "
R. K. Casper, " " " "
D. S. C. Jones, " " " "
J. C. Grady, " " " "
J. B. Twyner, 3rd " " "

Near this monument are six small stones each inscribed C. S. A. May 5th, 1662; and three stones inscribed as follows:
    C. S. A., St. John Addison, Co. G., 17th Va. Regt.,
                May 5th, 1662.
C. S. A., Capt. A. J. Humphreys, Co. A., 17th Va. Regt., Killed at the Battle of Williamsburg, May 5th, 1662.
C. S. A.   C. T. W.

Names Engraved on Tomb-Stones in Bruton Church and Church Yard, with Date of Death

Michael Archer, 1726; Joana Archer, 1732; Thomas Hugh Nelson Burwell, 1841; Rolandus Jones, clericus, 1688; David Meade Randolph, 1830; Hon. John Blair, 1800; John Millington, 1868; his mother-in-law, Mrs. Elizabeth Lett, 1847; Sidney Smith, 1881; Virginia C. Smith, 1878; Delia Adalaide Bucktrout, 1857; Josiah Nelson Bucktrout, 1836; Richard Manning Bucktrout, 1847; Horatio Nelson Bucktrout, 1854; Lulie E. Dugger, 1870; Benjamin Earushaw Bucktrout, 1846; Benjamin Bucktrout, 1849; Mrs. Catherine Stephenson, 18(32?); H. S. E. Edwardus Barradall Armiger, 1743; Henricus Barradall, 1737; children of Henry Washington and his wife, Cynthia Beverly Tucker, Lucy 1854; Sarah Augustine, 1862;

Catherine Brooks Coleman, 1883; Annie B. Gilliam, 1900; Mary Westwood, 1869; Mrs. Ann Burgess, 1771; Catharine Stith, 1776; Mrs. Catharine Blackley, 1771; James Grinsley, 1763; Robt. H. Hord, 1845; James Dix, 1861; John Blair, 1792; James Blair, 1791; Edward B. Lindsay, 1855; Jane Blair Henderson, 1800; James Blair Henderson, 1795; John Blair Henderson, 1797; Blair Monroe Henderson, 1801; George Bascom Lindsay, 1860; Mr. Charles Hunt, 1794; Sarah Lindsay, 1850; John Greenhow, 1787; Elizabeth Greenhow, 1781; Judith Greenhow, 1765; Mrs. Francis Custis, 17$\frac{14}{15}$; Daniel Parke Custis, 1754; Francis Parke Custis, 1757; Elizabeth Henderson, 1813; Revd. James Henderson, 1818; Thomas Hamilton Henderson, 1814; Elizabeth Bingham, 1851; Ann B. Wilmer, 1854; Captain Francis Page, 1692; Alice Page, 1698; John Collett, 1749; Mrs. Mary Francis Page, 169–; Col. John Page, 169$\frac{1}{2}$; Thomas Hornsby, 1772; Mrs. Margaret Hornsby, ——; Margaret Brown, 1720; Jane Brown, 1720; Thomas Lyttleton Savage, 1855; Lauretta Ann Winder, 1879; Mary Nicolson, 1793; Thomas Ludwell, Esq., 1678; Mary E. Dixon, 1836; Elizabeth Page, 1702; Col. David Bray, 1717; Mrs. Judith Bray, 1720; David Bray, Armiger, 1731; Elizabeth Bray, 1734; James Bray, 1690; Joseph Scrivener, 1772; James Whaley, 1701; Mathew Whaley, 1705; Capt. Thomas Thorp, 1693; Katherine Thorp, 1695; Edward Dyer, 1722; Ann Charlton, 17(44?); Mrs. Eliza Williams, 1829; Hugh Orr, 1764; John Yuille, 1746; Seth Sewell Briggs, 1812; Susand L. W. Briggs, 1811; Mary M. Dehart, 1839; John W. Wyatt, 1849; Margaret F. Clows, 1853; Ann Snow, 1855; John L. Tilford, 1862; Mary L. McCann, 1846; Rev. Scervant Jones, 1854; Mrs. Ann Timson Jones, 1849; Millicent Jones, 1751; Mrs. Anne Frank, 1759; Robert Major Garrett, 1885, and Susan C. Winder, his wife, 1854; Henry Winder Garrett, 1879; Robert Winder Garrett, 1838; Comfort Anna Garrett, 1854; S. C. Garrett, 1878; Thomas O. Cogbill, 1858; Mrs.

Tomb-stone Inscriptions

Virginia Abbott, 1830; James Cabaniss, 1837; Robt. Rae, 1753; His Excellency Edward Nott, 1706; Mrs. Mary Purdie, 1772; Mrs. Sarah Griffin, 1846; Lady Christina Stuart, 1807; James Nicolson, 1773; Judge Nathl. Beverly Tucker, 1851; Mrs. Lucy Ann Tucker, 1867; Reuben Smith, 1843; Margaret W. Durfey, 1865; Altazera E. Durfey, 1835; Thomas G. Durfey, 1847; Mr. Orlando Jones, 1681; the Confederate dead (see Memorial page.)

The tomb-stones give no indication as to the number of persons buried in the church-yard. Many of the old stones have been broken, and the fragments scattered. As far as possible these will be collected and placed in the tower floor for preservation. Over the larger portion of the church yard the graves are unmarked by either monument or mound. In the spring fresh flowers grow over them, and in the winter they lie covered with leaves of autumn, or beneath an unsullied mantle of snow.

Tomb=stone Inscriptions—Addenda

Richard Southgate, 1828; Mrs. Mary Arnet Galt, 1854; Emily Morrison, 1887; Richard Kemp, Esqr., and Sr. Thomas Lunsford, Kt.; these two names are inscribed on the tomb of Thomas Ludwell, (See p. 104.)

For names inscribed on Mural Tablets, See Tablet Inscriptions, pp. 88-92.

Appendix C
List of the Ministers of Bruton Parish

Rowland Jones, 1674-1688——Samuel Eburne, 1688-1697——Cope Doyley, 1697-1702——Solomon Wheatley, 1702-1710——James Blair, 1710-1743——Thomas Dawson, 1743-1759——William Yates, 1759-1764——James Horrocks, 1764-1771——John Camm, 1771-1773——John Bracken, 1773-1818——R. Keith, D. D., 1821-1824——William H. Wilmer, 1826-1827——Adam Empie, 1828-1836——William Hodges, D. D., 1837-1848——Henry M. Denison, 1848-1852——George Wilmer, D. D., 1856——Thomas M. Ambler, 1860-1873——George Wilmer, D. D. (2d pastorate), 1872-1876——Jacquelin Meredith, 1876-1877——Henry Wall, S. T. D., 1877-1880——Alexander Overby, 1880-1885——F. G. Burch, 1885-1887——Lyman B. Wharton, D. D., 1888——T. C. Page, 1889-1893——W. T. Roberts, 1894-1902——W. A. R. Goodwin, 1903.

Partial List of the Vestry of Bruton Parish

[The dates represent their first appearance in the records].

1674.—Hon. Daniel Parke, Hon. John Page, James Besouth, Robert Cobbs, James Bray, Capt. Philip Chesley, William Aylett. 1679—George Poindexter, George Martin. 1682—Major Otho Thorpe, Capt. Francis Page. 1684—Hon. Philip Ludwell, Hon. Thomas Beale. 1686—Martin Gardner. 1694—Hon. Edmund Jenings, John Dormar, William Pinkethman, Hugh Norvell, Henry Tyler, John Kendall, Robert Crawley, Baldwin Mathews. 1697—John Owens, Philip Ludwell, Jr., Timothy Pinkethman. 1704—William Hansford, Joseph White, William Timson. 1705—Frederick Jones, John Page. 1710—Richard Kendall, Ambrose Cobbs, Richard Bland, David Bray. 1721—Mathew Pierce, John Holloway, John Custis, Michael Archer, Robert Cobbs, Jr., Henry Cary, Dr. Archibald Blair. 1725—Lewis Burwell. 1727 Sir John Randolph. 1744—James Wray, Hon. John Blair, Sr., John Harmer, Benjamin Waller. 1747—Hon. Peyton Randolph. 1750—John Holt. 1754—Robert Carter Nicholas. 1761—Frederick Bryan. 1769—Thomas Everard, John Pierce, William Eaton, George Wythe, John Prentis, William Graves.

The following names are taken from Meade's *Old Churches*, as occurring in the old vestry book which ended in 1769: Hon. Thomas Ludwell, Hon. Thomas Ballard, James Vaulx, William Corker, Thomas Whaley, Capt. Thomas Williams, Daniel Wyld, Thomas Taylor, Christopher Pearson, Gideon Macon, Robert Spring, Abraham Vincler, Samuel Timson, Thomas Pettus, Col. Thomas Ballard, Ralph Graves, Capt. James Archer, George Norvell, Edward Jones, Capt. Thomas Thorpe, Daniel Park, Jr., James Whaley, James Bray, James Hubard, Nathaniel Crawley, John Clayton, David Bray, Jr., Thomas Jones, Samuel Turner, George Nicholas, William Robertson, Thomas Cobbs, Ralph Graves, Edward Barradall, Jr., **James Barber, Daniel Needler, James Bray,**

Jr., Edward Barradall, Jr., Henry Tyler, Jr., Mathew Pierce, William Parks, William Prentis, William Timson, Jr., Armistead Burwell, John Palmer, Pinkethman Eaton, Nathaniel Shields, John Power.

Vestrymen from 1827-1853

Henry Edloe, Jesse Cole, John Page, Dr. Thomas G. Peachy, Dr. —— Griffin, W. W. Webb, James Semple, Sr., Robert McCandlish, Burwell Bassett, William Waller, Leonard Henley, Ferdinand S. Campbell, Judge James Semple, Thomas Coleman, Chas. L. Wingfield, James Cabaniss, J. C. Sheldon, Richard M. Bucktrout, Henley Taylor, Robert P. Waller, William B. Rodgers, Roscow Cole, William Edloe, Robert Saunders, Judge B. Tucker, John Millington, A. G. Southall, Dickie Galt, R. —— Randolph, John B. Christian, John Coke, Thomas E. Evans, G. —— Durfey, Doctor R. M. Garrett, J. M. Maupin, William W. Vest, Joseph Walker, William Waller, John M. Galt, J. T. Christian, John A. Henley, Joshua Walker, Jr.

Vestrymen from 1865-1903

From 1853 to 1865 there is no record.
1865-1903. Robert Saunders, P. Montague Thompson, W. W. Vest, R. F. Cole, J. O. Mumford, Dr. Robert Garrett, Mr. E. Taliaferro, Richard Hansford, G. Durfey, William S. Peachey, John A. Henley, Benjamin S. Ewell, R. T. Armistead, H. T. Jones, Jr., Robert A. Bright, Dr. D. R. Brower, John L. Mercer, C. W. Coleman, W. L. Wall, W. H. E. Morecock, Sydney Smith, Van F. Garrett, John L. Mercer, H. L. Hundley, C. C. Dixon, J. R. Copeland, B. D. Peachy, L. W. Lane, Jr., Leonard Henley, Jr., Dr. J. D. Moncure, Dr. John Clopton, John Spencer, J. B. C. Spencer, Dr. E. G. Booth, J. L. Hall, H. D. Cole, Dr. H. A. Wise, Dr. A. V. I. Deekens, J. T. Christian, J. C. Pilkinton, Dr. P. T. Southall, E. W. Warburton, Dr. L. S. Foster, Dr. W. P. Hoy, W. C. Johnson, T. G. Peachy, W. H. Macon.

TWO PAGES OF THE OLD PARISH REGISTER.

Appendix D
Birth Record

The birth record in the old Parish register extends from 1739 to 1797. The cost of printing the details of this record would have been very great. We have therefore copied, and now print tor the first time, this record giving simply a complete list of the names contained therein, with the dates under which they appear. The Christian name is given first, separated by a comma from the names of the parents. Where the date does not immediately precede the name, the date last given is the one under which it appears in the record book.

The names of slaves, or servants, baptized, with the names of their owners, have not been printed. Thirty-three consecutive pages in the register are filled with the record of the baptism of slaves, or negro servants, as they are generally called. This record shows that from 1747 to 1790 one thousand and forty-nine of these servants were baptized into the Church. Besides these there are many entries of such baptisms on the pages of the book not specifically set apart for this special record. One of the pages photographed from this old Parish register contains the record of some of these baptisms. An examination of this portion of the register shows that the prominent men of that day, such as George Washington, Sir John Randolph, Peyton Randolph, Governor Francis Fauquier, and others, took pains to see that their servants were brought under the influence and care of the Church.

*1739—John, George and Elizabeth Holden——Susanna, Dudley and Mary Diggs——James, James and Ann Shields ——John, John and Rebecca Coulthard——John, Wm. and Elizabeth Highland——John, Joseph and Ann Maples—— Ann, Kenneth and Joannah McKenzie——Richard, Thomas and Jane Wade——William, Mary Haython——Richard,

---
*The spelling used in the Old Register is adhered to, though often incorrect and inconsistent. The abbreviation bap. signifies baptized.

John and Sarah Coke——Elizabeth, Richard and Christian Giles——Lucy, Wm. and Ann Keith——Mary, Robert and Adling Fry.

1740—Mathew, Thomas and Ann Holt——Francis, Francis and Frances Durphey——Margaret Mekinin Wells.

1741—Easter, John and Mary Page——Elizabeth, James and Eliz. Byrd——Richard Wells and 1744, George Wells, George and Elizabeth Wills——Susanna Peachy, George Gilmer——John, John and Hannah Taylor——Sukey, David and Eliz. Force——James, John and Betty Foy——1741, Mary, Mark and Mary Cosby.

1742—Elizabeth, George and Ann Jude——Judith, Thomas and Eliz. Dickinson——Ann, James and Ann Shields.

1743—Jane, James and Eliz. Byrd——John, Thomas and Ann Holt——1742, Judith, Thomas and Eliz. Dickinson——1741, John, John and Mary Carter——1743, Elizabeth, John and Mary Carter——Catharine, Wm. and Eliz. Wyatt——1733, Francis, Cliffen and Sarah Rhodes——1735, Ann, Cliffen and Sarah Rhodes——1737, Sarah, Cliffen and Sarah Rhodes——1740, Rebecca, Cliffen and Sarah Rhodes——1743, Cliffen, Cliffen and Sarah Rhodes——Barbary, Thomas and Sarah Atkins——1743, Robert, Andrew and Mary Anderson.

1744—Lucretia, Robert and Adling Fry——Sarah, James and Tabytha Barden——Archibald, Hon. John and Mary Blair——Anne, Alexander and Susanna Reed——1745, Elizabeth, Dennis and Mary Mourning——William, Edward and Mary Maynard——1744, William, Benjamin and Eliz. Hansel——Elizabeth, John and Mary Green——John, George and Ann Jude——Sarah, James and Ann Geady——Elizabeth, Daniel and Rachel McIntosh——James, John and Mary Glass——Archibald, Hon. John and Mary Blair——Mildred, Godfrey and Mary——John, David and Joannah Esco.

1745—Thomas, Thomas and Eliz. Dickinson——Fyss, Fyss and Frances Jackson——William, John and Eliz.

Birth Record

Rawley——John, Joseph and Ann Cock——Ann, James and Eliz. Davis——Rebecka, Wm. and Eliz. Wellings——Hannah Harrison, James and Mary Wray——Mary, Richard and Ann Normand——Robey, John and Sarah Coke——Sarah, Thomas and Mary Cobbs——Bethiah, James and Eliz. Byrd——Susanna, John and Mary Page——Waller, Thomas and Eliz. Jones.

1746—William, Kenneth and Joannah McKenzie—— Robert, Robt. and Eliz. Stevenson——Elizabeth, Thos. and Eliz. Holt——Frances, Geo. and Mary Camp—— William, Wm. and Mary Nichols——Susannah, John and Susannah Lane——Susannah, Dudley and Mary Diggs—— Christianna, James and Ann Shields——Weary, or Mary, Geo. and Sarah Russel——David, Abraham and Eliz. Roberts——Tabytha, Jas. and Tabytha Barden—— Elizabeth, David and Lucy Musgroves——Elizabeth, James and Eliz. Davis——1746, John, Revd. Thos. and Editha Robinson——John, Thomas and Sarah Atkins——Archibald, Hon. John and Mary Blair——1745, Lewis, Armistead and Christian Burwell——174-, Judith, John and Judith Brown——1746, John, Armistead and Christian Burwell ——Ann, Hon. John and Mary Blair——Pamelia, Thos. and Ann Holt——David and Davis, twins, James and Eliz. Renolds——William Waters, Wm. and Mary Bradford—— Martha, Man and Martha Bryan——Robert, Benj. and Eliz. Hansel——Mary, Thos. and Eliz. Dickinson—— Mathew, Daniel and Eliz. Harmpeld, or Harmfield——Mary Robinson, John and Elizabeth Rawlison——William, Thos. and Anne Wilkins——1747, James, James and Mary Wray ——Jacob, Severinus and Mary Durfey, of James City at that time——1732, Elizabeth, Serverinus and Mary Durfey, 1736, Samuel, ditto——1738, Francis, ditto——1741, Serverinus, ditto——1741, John, John James and Mary Hulett——1744, Elizabeth, ditto——1745, Martha, ditto ——1749, Mary, ditto.

1747—Martha, Benjamin and Martha Waller—— Thomas, Thos. and Rachel Robinson——1748, Mary, Dr.

Kennith and Joana McKenzie——1747, Anne, James and
Eliz. Oats.

1748—John, Dennis and Mary Moring——1748,
Elizabeth, Fips Jackson——1748, bap. James, David
Musgrove——bap. Frances, James and Frances Davis——
John, Wm. and Anne Davenport——Elizabeth, Planey
Ward——bap. John, George and Sarah Russel——bap.
Mary, Revd. Thomas and Editha Robinson——Henry,
Joseph James——1748, John and Elizabeth, twins, Daniel
and Frances Hughs——bap. Dudley, Dudley and Mary
Digges——Hannah, Thos. Atkins——Anne, John and ——
Back——bap. Johny Peters, Anthony Jaspar——
Pinkethman, Pinkethman and Mary Eaton——Edward
Cross, Edw. and Mary Maynard——Sarah, John and
Anne Bell.

1749—Elizabeth, Peter and —— Morrow, a French
Man——Robert, Benjamin and Martha Waller——William,
Robt. and Mary Nicolson——Alexander, George Jones and
Margaret Maeplin——John, James and Eliz Wilson, (late
Eliz. Alexander)——Thomas, Thos. and Anne Wilkins.

1750—Benjamin, Benjamin and Martha Waller——
Elizabeth, James and Elizabeth Wilson——Agnes Rutton,
Thos. and Eliz. Dickinson——Joseph, P. Nehemiah and
Caroline Hunley——John, Jno. and Judith Brown——
Rebecca, Wm. and Rebecca Rice——Abigail, James and
Anne Oats——Alexander, Geo. Jones and Margaret McKlin.

1751—Nancy, John and Anne Wright——Dixon Brown,
John and Mary Peal——John, Robt. and Mary Nicolson
——John Hubard, Seth and Eliz. Watkins——Elizabeth,
Edw. and Mary Maynard——Samuel, Thos. and Anne
Wilkins——Daniel, Daniel and Frances Hughes——Frances,
Ashwell and Mary Stone, of New Kent Co.——Robert,
Thos. and Lucy Stevens.

1752—Anne, Wm. and Eliz. Timson——Barbara,
Anthony and Elizabeth Hay, (late Eliz. Penman)——
William, Wm. and Mary Davenport——Martha, James and
Eliz. Wilson——Molly, William and Molly Dunn——

Birth Record

Elizabeth, Thos. and Mary Withers——Martha, Benjamin and Martha Waller——Manettrel, Thos. and Bette Jones——Thomas, Thomas and Hannah Jones.

1753—Sarah, Richard and Mary Singleton——1752, Joseph, John and Eliz. Curtis——1753, William, Wm. and Lydia Richeson——Robert, Edw. and Mary Maynard——Hannah, Benj. and Anabella Powell——Jane, Robt. and Anne Crawley——Henry, Wm. and Judy Bray, Armistead——Elizabeth, Thomas and Eliz. Dickinson——Jane, John and Catherine Didip, wife of late Cathanne Marshall——William, Nehemiah and Caroline Hunley——Ambrose, Ambrose and Sarah Jackson——Robert, Robt. and Mary Nicolson.

1754—Elizabeth, James and Mary Oates——Joseph Seagrove, Nathaniel, Sr., and Sarah Crawley——Thomas, Anthony and Eliz. Hayes——Naomi, Thos. and Mette Jones.

1757—William, John and Hannah Rhodes——Anne, Wm. and Mary Davenport——Thomas and Samuel, sons, John and Mary Bartle.

1758—Molly, Peter and Eliz. Powell——Susannah, Wm. and Susannah Green——William Bosawan, Wm. and Mary Rose——Thomas Thorp, Graham and Anne Frank——1757, George, Robt. and Mary Nicolson——1758, Thomas, Rebecca Bird, wd.

1759—John, James Matt. and Anne Ince——James, James and Lucy Atherton——Thomas, Thomas and Anne Craig——Mary, John and Mary Bendall——John Bond, Daniel and Ann Hoge——1761, Repceme, ditto——1764, Nancy, ditto——1758, John, Wm. and Eliz. Pearson——1759, Mary Barden, Simpin and Jane Bryan——Mary, George and Mary Powell——1758, Sally Armistead, John and Judith Brown——Sarah, John and Anne Bell——John, Frederick and Barbary Bryan——1758, Joseph, Anthony and Eliz. Hay, late Elizabeth Davenport——1759, Adam, James and Anne Craig, late Anne Stephenson——William, John Nathan and Anne Carter——1761, Elizabeth, James and Anne Taylor, (Shoemaker)——1759, Mary, Wm. and Mary Davenport——Hellen, John, Jr. and Jane Blair—— 1760, Anne, John and Rachael Warrington——James, John Carter——Lucy, Abraham and Ann Cole——1759, John, John and Rachael Warrington——George, John and Mary Chowning——Thomas, John and Jane Carter, late Jane Mitchell——Frederick, Frederick and Barbara Bryan——1758, David Bringley, Joseph and Eliz. Wade—— 1761, Thomas, George and——Powell——Robt., John and Judith Greenhow——1759, Catharine, Christopher and Ann Ayscough.

1760—Frances, ditto——1762, Ann, ditto——1763, Margaret, ditto——1765, Edward, ditto——1767, Clary, ditto——1762, Elizabeth, Wm. and Mary Holt——1764, Daniel, ditto——1762, William Stith, William and Elizabeth Pasteur——Sarah, John and Elizabeth Barnes ——1763, John, James and Francis Southall——Judith, Samuel and Judith Coke——1763, Ann J(?)asker, Robert and Francis Carter——1764, Francis, Hon. Robert and Frances Carter——Ann, Henry and Martha Bolton—— John, James and Elizabeth Bell, 1763——1762, Angelyca, George and Margret Lafong——1763, John, John and Francis Ormiston——1762, Thomas, Francis and Elizabeth Durfey——1764, Francis, Francis and Elizabeth Durfey—— 1764, Ann, James and Ann Craig, (Jeweler)——1766, James, ditto.

1765—Nancy, William and Mary Stone——Francis, Frederick and Barbary Bryan——Mary, Alexander and Barbara Hoye——Peter, Peter and Elizabeth Powell—— 1765, Frances, William and Ann Graves——Elizabeth, Edward and Mary Haynes——Ann, William and Ann Jackson——Sarah, Samuel and Judith Coke——Robert, John and Frances Ormeston——Dixson, Robert and Ann Bond——William, William and Mary Holt——William, Mathew, Jr., and Katherine Moody —— Elizabeth, Humphrey and Sarah Harwood——Samuel, James and Mary Galt——Betty Landon, Hon. Robert and Frances

Birth Record

Carter——Elizabeth, Benjamin and Sally Eggleston—— Henry, Richard and Dinnah Street——Chritian, John, Jun., and Jane Blair——Jennet, Alixander and Mary Purdy—— George, Anthany and Eliz. Hay——Sally, Benjamin and Martha Waller——1766, Mary, Gabriel and Easter Maupin ——1765, Hunter, Joseph and Roseama Royle——Arenna, Wm. and Ann Saunders.

1766—Jonny Wyate, Edward and Martha Westmore ——Elizabeth, James and Eliz. Holdcraft——Phillip, James and Frances Southall——Mary, Samuel and Lucy Trower ——Mary, James and Eliz. Geddy——Mary, William and Mary Pearson——John, John and Eliz. Sheppard—— Elizabeth, William and Eliz. Phillips——Mary Symmer Degliesh, Wm. and Susanna Roberts.

(Page out of place in Record Book) 1762—Sarah, William and Mary Davenport——William, Benj. and Martha Waller——John, Samuel and Judith Coke——Ann, Thomas and Ann Blasingham——George, Peter and Rebecca Mires——John, Robert and Ann Bond——Fanny, William and Ann Jackson——Edward, John and Anne Bell——bap. Susanna, Benj. and Charity Ricket——1763, bap. Katherine, Thomas and Katherine Dunn——bap. Elizabeth and Rebecca, Mathew and Eliz. Doran——Mary, John and Rachel Warrington——James, Wm. and Rebecca Carter——John, Walter and Eliz. Lenox——Ann, John and Jane Carter——1758, Joseph Mathews, George and Katherine Davenport——1760, Anne, ditto——1763, John, Peter and Ann Pelham——James, Wm. and Eliz. Reynolds ——1764, Robert Hall, Benj. and Martha Waller——1763, Andrew, Robert and Mary Nicolson——1764, Rebecca, John and Rachael Warrington——Elizabeth, John and Jane Carter——Elizabeth Craton——George William, Wm. and Anna Bradley——Elizabeth, John and Mary Bendall—— Mary Elizabeth, Peter and Rebecca Moyer——William Allen, Walther and Eliz. Lenox——Newton, John and Mouning Connilly——James, James and Frances Southall ——176-, Patrick, Robert and Mary Highland——176-,

William, ditto——1765, Elizabeth Meakings, John and Mary White——Nancy, Wm. and Eliz. Finnie——Ann, Wm. and Mary Magdalene Pearson——Elizabeth, Wm. and Jenny Dennis——William, Wm. and Rebecca Carter—— William, Simon and Rachel Whittaker——1764, William, Mungo and Sarah Campbell——1765, Sarah, Eliz. and Richard Basset——John, James and Mary Black——Ann, James and Susana Shields——Edward, John and Martha Hennese——Joseph, Wm. and Mary Davenport——William, John and Eliz. Barns——James, James and Frances Hubard——Ann, Richard and Sarah Brown——Archibald, Wm. and Mary Rose——Mary, Chas. and Sarah Porter—— Mary, John and Eleanor Seagrove Camp——William Sealy Lano, William Sealy and Courtney Lano——Judith, Robert Carter and Ann Nicholas——William, William and Eliz. Bland.

1766—Polly, Wm. and Mary Rose —— Elizabeth, George and Mary Arnest——John, James Eliz. Bryan—— James, Wm. and Rebecca Carter——Rebecca, Robert and Mary Nicolson——Jane, Rich. and Sarah Charlton——Cary Mitchell, John and Jane Carter——Mathew Mallory, Mathew and Kathern Moody——George, George and Margret Lafong——Lewis, Robert Carter and Ann Nicholas——George, John and Eleanor Seagrove Camp—— John, John and Mouning Connilly——Sarah, Alixander and Mary Craig——Robert Timson, Robert and Mary Highland——William, Rowland and Sarah Crone—— Thomas, Walter and Eliz. Lenox——Mathew, James and Frances Hubard.

1767—William, James and Hannah Anderson—— Elizabeth, James and Eliz. Bell——William, Robert and Ann Bond——John Grierson, William and Clementine Rind ——John McCarty, Wm. Sealy and Courtney Lane—— ——, Alexander and Mary Purdy——Sarah, Richard and Dianna Street——Robert, Tomkins and Martha Martyr ——Richard, Abraham and Ann Cole——A son of James and Frances Southall——Elizabeth, George and Eliz.

Birth Record 129

Wilson——Ann, John and Mary Dewbre——Mary, Hon. Robert and Frances Carter——Fanny, Benj. and Martha Waller——Sally, Richard and Sarah Brown——Mary, Jonathan and Mary Prosser——Francis, Francis and Eliz. Durfey——John, Edmond and Ann Sanders—— Elizabeth Jackson, John and Sarah Timson——John, John and Mary White——Lucretia, Edward and Mary Haynes ——Mary, John and Rachael Warrington——James Reynolds, Wm. and Mary Davenport.

1768—Benjamin, William and Martha Taylor——John, John and Eleener Segrove Camp——Ann Shields, Frederick, Jun. and Ann Bryan——Elizabeth, William and Mary Godfrey——William, Humphrey and Sarah Harwood—— 1767—Elizabeth, William and Mary Magdlen Pearson—— Anthony, Anthony and Eliz. Hay——1768, Benjamin, William and Eliz. Fear——Alixander, Alix. and Hannah Martin——Robert, Robert Carter and Ann Nicholas—— William Dawson, James and Ann Clayton——Charles, William and Clementine Rind——George, George and Cathern Aubrey Haynes——James, James and Eliz. Cocke ——Samuel, James and Eliz. Holdcraft——William, Blovet and Mary Pasteur——Harrison, Mathew and Kathrine Moody——Hariet Lucy, Hon. Robert and Frances Carter, Esq.——Mary, George and Mary Arnest——Rachel, William and Rachael Phillips——Robert, John and Mary Rattlif ——Jane How, William and Rebecca Carter——John Tyler, James and Hannah Anderson——Mary, John and Anne Earnshaw——Charlott, Robert and Ann Bond——Moses Russel, William Pearman——Mary, Steven and Martha May——Sarah, James and Betty Valantine——Randolph, Walther and Eliz. Lenox——Nathniel, William and Ann Saunders——Jane, Richard and Sarah Brown——A son of John and Roseanna Dixson——Meriwether, James and Frances Hubard——Nelley, John and Mouning Connilly ——1770, Humphrey, Humphrey and Sarah Harwood—— 177 , Robert, David and Mary Morton——Thomas, ditto ——Mary, ditto——David, ditto——1776, Anne Garland

Carr, William and Mary Goodson——1778, William Greenwood, ditto——1780, Samuel Spurr, ditto——177 , William, William and Eliz. Hunter——1777, Mary (?) Hewes, Henry Field——1779, **John, Revd. John and Sarah Bracken** ——Frances, Hunphey and Sarah Harwood——1780, John Meed, Wm. and Eliz. Lark——Christian, Druits, a Dane—— Ann, Charles and Eliz. Lisle——1781, Mary, Holeman and Sarah Minnis——John, Beverly and Mary Dickson—— Edward Smith, William and Ann Jiggits——John Rochanbeau, Philip and Judith Moody——John, John and Sarah Wright——Matilda Aylett, Saml. and Anne Beall ——Sarah, Philip and Rebecca Bullifant——Richard, Richard and —— Booker——Sally, Thomas and Sarah Bristow——Fanny, John and Anne Carter——Sylla and Sally, twins, Joseph and Frances Crawley——Molly, Ambrose and Sarah Jackson——Jane, William and Eliz. Russell——Nancy, Andrew and Mary Flax——Julia Carter, John and Sarah Bracken——Elizabeth Garland, William and Eleanor Pitt——Elizabeth, Hulitt and Jane Rollison ——Sarah Irebell, John M. and Judith Galt——1782, John, Saml. and Eliz. Dubree——John, William and Rebecca Bacon——1783, **Elizabeth and Robert, Rev. Robert and Eliz. Andrews**——John Craig, J. W. and Jane Shileds ——James, James and Mary Galt——Elizabeth, Henry and Eliz. Nicolson——Joseph, Joseph and Margret Prentis—— James, John and Mary Ratcliff——Catherine, John and Lucretia Blasingham——Betsey, Charles and Searbourough Orrel——William Swiney, William L. and Ann Bolton—— James, Joseph and Jane Wallace——Elizabeth, Daniel and Martha Dean——Polly, Chas. and Polly Graves——1784, Mary, Humphrey and Sarah Harwood——Mary Cosby, James and Eliz. Johnson——Thomas, John and Mary Jones——Thomas, Thomas and Esther Scot——Elizabeth Randolph, Robert and Lucy Sandford——Ann McKenzie, William and Eliz. Lark.

  1785—Gideon, John and Mary Ratcliff——Betsy, Saml. and Sarah Wright——Judith Bray Inglis, James and

Birth Record

Susanna Shield——Charlott, Saml. and Frances Able——William Chesley, John and Eliz. Roadman——Mary Wilkinson, Thomas and Eliz. Cowles——William, Wm. and Eliz. Dick——Christianna, John and Marg. Stokes——William Farrow, Wm. and Eliz. Russell——William, Joseph and Margaret Prentis——Warren Ware, Eliz. Lyon——William Beverly, Thomas and Sarah Bristow——Martha, Wm. and Rebecca Baker——Ann Brown, James and Eliz. Innis——Jane Wright, Duncan and Margaret McPherson ——Elizabeth, John S. Alix. and Eliz. Besserer——John Minson, James and Mary Galt——Jane, David and——Morton——Lucy Ann, John M. and Judith Galt——Humphrey Chase, John and Catherine Wright——Penelope Johnston, Walker and Mary Maury——Mary, John and Mary Reynolds——Eliza Trebell, William and Eliz. Finnie——Samuel, Samuel and Eliz. Dubree——William Taliaferro, William and Mary Nelson——Thomas, William and Mary Gibbs——Sarah, John and Sarah Bracken——Elizabeth, George and Ann Jackson——1786, James Solomon, James Solomon Cumbo and wife——Esther, Son, John and Susan Cole——1787, Elizabeth Cumbo, Solomon Cumbo and Wife——1790, Sarah Cumbo, ditto——1787, Richard, John and Mary Radcliff——Susanna, John and Susanna Cole ——Richard, James and Mary Galt——1789, Gabriel, ditto——1792, George, John and Mary Bray.

Appendix E

Death Record, 1662=1751

The following is a complete list of the names of those who are recorded as having died from 1662 to 1751, the names of slaves being omitted:

*1662—Bridgett, w. John Russell——Fielding, s. Capt. Daniel Parke —— Frances, w. Alexander Walker —— Vi(?)sley, w. Asael Batten.

1663—Mary, d. Garret Hawthorne——Robert, s. Mrs. Mary Walters——Elizabeth, w. William Gilbey——Mr. Tuley——Anne, w. Major Crenshaw——Robert Boyden—— Anne, d. Wm. and Jane Davis——Mary, d. Mr. Edwd. Foliott——John, s. John Davis——Daniel, s. Mr. Daniel Wylde——Daniel, s. Capt. Daniel Parke——Henry Phrodno ——Robert Thomas, s. John and Katherine Thomas—— Rachel, d, John and Mary Davis.

1664—Margaret, d. Henry White——Rebecca, d. Mr. Edward Foliot——John, s. John and Katherine Wells—— Mr Henry Banister——Richard and Robt., s. Valent Harvy——Margaret, w. Major Crenshaw——John Davis ——Elizabeth, d. John Johnson——Thomas Philip—— Nicholas Dunford——Katherine, w. John Wells——Thomas Austin, s. Mrs. Mary Bromfield——William Stone.

1665—John Evans——Captain Jeremiah Fisher—— Elizabeth, d. Daniel Wylde——Thomas Bromfield—— Thomas White——John Thomas——Adam, s. Elizabeth Strawhawne——Frances, d. Garret and Mary Hawthorne.

1666—James, s. James Wilkins——Robert Kempe—— Jane Berkley——Ann Luckey——Thomas Wilson——Asaell Batten —— Elizabeth Vaulx——William Jeph —— Henry Dennis——Elizabeth Davis——Martha Graves——Frances, d. Henry Binkfield——Thomas Predy——John Martin—— James Todeink (?)

1667—Major Joseph Creshaw——Adam Strawhun (?) ——Henry, s. Henry White——William Jackson——Ralph

*Abbreviations: S., son of. D., daughter of. W., Wife of.

Death Record

Graves——Edward Gwyn——John Morgan——John King ——Villerel (?) Hughs——Richard Todd——John Russell—— William Walthorne (?)——Robert Partridge——Katherine, d. Robert Partridge——Susan, w. Robert Hossington.

1668—Thomas, s. Thomas Penbethman——Thomas Wilkinson——George Woods——Hugh Cooper——Peter Sharpe——Mary, d. Mr. Graves——Sara, w. John Davis—— Benjamin, s. in law Thomas Holder——Mary, w. Thomas Holder——John, s. John Stephens——William, s. Daniel and Margaret Stephens——Elizabeth, w. James Trice, Samuel Crabtree——Ann, d. Rachell Graves——Katherine, w. Michaell Batos.

1669—Margaret, d. Capt. and Eliz. Crenshaw——Capt. Crenshaw——Rachell, w. Richard Barnes——John Cornon ——Martin Ireland —— Charles Hurst —— Rebecca, w. Francis Durphey——John, s. John and Mary Daniell—— Susanna, d. Daniel Somorton——Ann, d. Henry and Mary White —— Thomas Gregory —— Richard Whitehair —— James Wells——Daniell, s. Richard and Sarah Kempe.

1670—John Smith, William Phillips——Elizabeth, d. John and Eliz. Equo——Charles Wheeler——Ann, d. Anthony and Margaret Sands —— John Woods —— John Peters —— Jarret Hawthorne —— Frances, d. Capt. Francis Mathews.

1671—Thomas, s. in law Thomas Milton——Elizabeth, w. Thomas Whaley——William Hazell——Hannah, w. Cook——Marth, w. Jas. Bullock——Thomas, s. John and Jane Cole——Anthony, s. Anthony and Margaret Sands—— Richard, s. Ricd. and Eliz. Shurley——Elizabeth, d. Capt. Frances Mathews——Sarah, d. Wm. and Eliz. Tucker—— Lettie, d. Rite and Eliz. Jones——Edward, s. Edwd. and Bridget Ivory——William Lancaster——Joan, w. Thomas Penkethman——Paul Johnson Clark——Henry White—— Robert Horsington——Jrauna, d. Frances Gutteridge—— Anne Lee, w. Henry Bingfield——Dorothy, d. Anthony Sands——John Horsington.

1672—William, s. Cornelius Jonathan——Robert, s.

134   Death Record

Clement Mash——Martha, w. Robert Robinson——Mr. Clement Marsh——Mr. Thomas Penckethman.
1673—Susanna, w. Francis Durfey——Margaret, w. Anthony Sands——Mary, d. Capt. Francis Mathews——William Haskett.
1674—William Bell —— Robert Wharton —— Mary Simpkins——James Bisit——Valentine Harvey——John, s. James Bisit——Sebella Aylett——Capt. Philip Chesley——Thomas Simpkins——Henry Townsend——Richard Turner Richard Barnes——Henry Taylor——Thomas, s. James Vaulx —— Julian Davis, widow——Edward Bray —— Francis Mathews.
1675—James Field——Dorothy, w. Capt. Otho Thorp ——John Wattles——Mary, w. John Wattles——George Jude, Sexton——Elizabeth, w. Robert Bee——Hunphrey Veale——Robert, s. Capt. Anthony Archer——Margaret Wylde——Elizabeth, w. Capt. Thorp——Elizabeth, w. Samuel Richardson——Anne Jackson——Capt. William Corker——Mr. Lewis Griffin——John Dickinson——William Gilbey.
1676—John Rogers, Sr.——John Frederick——Gyles Rogers——William Thomas——Thomas Sturgis——George Bates——John Scot——Thomas Rentmore.
1677 — James Vaulx —— William Tantey —— John Russell——Elizabeth Hutchins——Capt. Thomas Williams ——Thomas Sampson.
1678 — Thomas Wilkinson —— Anna, w. Thomas Ballard, Esq.——William Aylett——John Wisdem (?)——Adam Hudson——Elizabeth, w. Rowland Jones, Clark——Thomas Wilkinson——Warrick Haile——The Honourable Thomas Ludwell——Adam Hudson——The Hon. Daniel Parke——Mary, w. Christopher Peirson——Nicholas Toop.
1679—Mary, w. Nicholas Toop——Anne, w. Martin Gardner——Edward Bessy.
1680—John, s. Richard Saint——Robert Simpson——Alice, w. John Dormar——James Cooper——Mathew Edwards.

Death Record

1681—James Besouth——Samuel, s. Samuel Timson——John Bell——William Fellows——Anne, w. Richard Haley.

1682—Mr. Gwinn——Joseph Crenshaw——Mrs. Lydia Aylett, widow——Joan, w. Thomas Mille——William Gravenor——Edward, s. Nicholas Sebrill——Robert Cobbe——Robert Spring.

1683—Robert Prichard——Elizabeth, d. Capt. James Archur——Ambrose Cobbe——Margaret Porter——Morris Herd——James, s. John Taylor——James Wilkinson.

1684—Abraham, s. John Vadin——John, s. John Vadin——Anne Winchcom——Robert Handy——Thomas, s. Nicholas Sebrill——Henry, s. Henry Tyler——Mrs. Robt. Cobbs——Humphrey, s. Robert Lounsdale—— , s. Edward Jones, Merchant——Thomas Owen.

1685—Anne, w. Charles Digby——Richard Aynsley, Arthur Juxton——Margaret, w. Andrew Cole——Susanna, w. Job Corking——William Oxley.

1686—George Hewbank——Jane, w. Edward Jones Katherine, w. Henry Brower —— Joseph Bascom —— Margaret Bell——Rebecca White——Thomas Broad——Dorcas, w. William Atwood——Thomas Summers——George Norvell——Edward Davis——Anne, w. Edward Davis——Evan Owen——Christopher Walter——William Martin——Elizabeth, w. Thomas Jeffreys——Sarah Hale——Margaret Owen——Constant, w. William Davis——Edward Wadsworth——Edward Evans——Anne, d. John Teddar——John Garland——George Bridges——Leonard Dickeson——James Brand——Thomas Rogers——Vinty, w. George Robison——John, s. John Bates.

1687—Mr. Valentine Evans —— John Stevens —— Richard Peirse——Robert Miller——George Burkey, a Dutchman——Sarah Gilbert——Sarah, w. Edward Gyles Joan, w. John Meeke——John Whiting——Richard Crooke——Joan, w. Wm. Jackson——Margaret, w. William Kerle——Mary, w. Thomas Taylor——Joan, d. William Jackson——Elizabeth, d. Thomas Fear——Thomas Limb

——William Irish——William Preston——Esther Gold——
William Davis, Sen.——Robert Partridge——John Philips——
William Johnson.
    1688—**Mr. Rowland Jones, Clarke**——George Hewbank,
s. Geo. Hewbank——Mary, d. Geo. Hewbank——Abott, s.
Wm. Atwood——Mr. John Daniel——Isaac Goding——
William Rice——John Evans.
    1689—William Watson——Mary, w. Robert West——
John Harrison——Thomas Gorham——Thomas Ballard,
Esq.——George Glascock——Samuel Bainton.
    1690—Henry, s. Joseph White——Benett Casement,
widow——Alice, Edw. Giles——John, s. Mr. George Martin
——Edward Jones, Merchant——James Drake——William
Robison —— Mary, w. Capt. Francis Page —— John
Horsoon or Horvoor (?)——Jane, w. Robert Stanyard.
    1691—Mary Whiting——Anne, w. Wm. Coman——
Edmund Ivory——Elizabeth, d. Thos. Mills——John
Cooper——James Bray, Esq.——John Williams, a School
M. —— Anne, d. Edmund Jenings, Esq., —— Susanna
Ludbrook——John Page, Esq.——Robert Huellin.
    1692—Joan Hammer——Capt. Francis Page——Mary
Mills——Jane Hortshorn——Nicholas Sebrill, Sen.——
Geverge, s. Capt. Geo. Ravenscroft——Capt. Thomas
Thorp——Thomas Steward——William Iserell——Thomas
Bray——John Taylor——John Hopkins——John Clarke
——Mr. Nichols——Anne, w. James Harrison——Henry
Binkfield——Thomas Tibbs——Mr. Robert Jones——
Thomas Yates —— Richard Page —— Mrs. Katherine
Besouth —— Elizabeth, d. Richard Page —— John, s.
Christopher Peirson——Thomas Batts——Mr. Robert
Higgison——Evan Roberts——Joice, w. John Bates——
Elizabeth, d. John Bates——William Green——Mr. Edmund
Cobbs——John Keen——Mary Sutor.
    1693—Mary Keen, widow——Thomas, s. Christopher
Peirson——Mr. Martin Gardner——Sarah, w. Daniel
Hornby——Roan——Graves——Corville—— , wife of
L. Philip Wells.

1695—Vinity, w. Tho. Crips——John Spelman——Watson, widow——Robert Clarke——Jervas Newton.

1696—**Mr. Hudson, a minister**——Evelyn, d. Dan. Parke, Esq.——White, d. Joseph White——John Batten——George Jude——James, s. Wm. Kerle——John Brookman——John Turner——Thomas Mills——Mary, w. Timo. Pinketham——Rice Jones.

1694—Daniel Mecarte——Mr. Philip Wells——James Knell Cordwainer——Elenor Anderson——James Gibson——Elizabeth Crocus——William Graves——John Pollard——Alice Whitby——John Teddar——John Manly——Mr. Samuel Timson——Henry Goodwin——Mr. Peter Temple of Hampton Parish.

1695—Alexander Bonyman, Jr.——Mrs. Katherine Thorp——Elizabeth, d. Mr. Henry Tyler.

1701—**Mary, w. Rev. Mr. Cope Doyley, Clarke**——Mr. James Whaley, late Church-warden——Mr. Wickham——Joan, w. Thomas Tandy——Thomas Thorpe——**Mr. Allardis, minister**——Francis Durfy——Mrs. Lydia Vinkler, widow——Mr. John Kendall——Mr. Martin, merchant——Mr. Dowson——Susanna, w. Wm. White——Matthew, s. Nicho. Sebrill——Mr. John Owens.

1699—Elenor, w. Alexander Bonyman, Clerc. of this parish —— Robert Brooks —— John Stafford —— John Bonyman——Peter Johnson——Magdalen, w. Jos. White——Edward Davis——Edmund Pines——Susanna Evans——Thomas Teer——Robert Haley.

1700-1—William Jackson——John Bates——**Elizabeth, d. Cope Doyley.**

1701-2—Thomas Clayton —— William Sanders —— Susanna, w. Hon. Brewer——Mr. Adrian Preston, writing master——Mrs. Mary Pinkethhman——Mary Clayton, widow——Mr. Harvy, a merchant——Elizabeth Shelburn——**The Reverend Mr. Cope Doyley**——Mrs. Mary Timson, widow——Elenor, d. Mary Bonyman——Ann Pynes, widow——Elizabeth, w. Mr. John Page—— , wife of Mr. Lawrence Green——Mary Teer, widow.

1702-3—Thomas Cobbs——Elizabeth, w. Mr. Henry
Tyler——Emanuel Desveer, a Portuguese——Mary Dyer.
1703—Francis, w. John Steward——William White, a
Planter —— Alberter Warren —— Margaret Bentley——
James, s. Wm. Harrison——Mr. George Martin——John
Web——Francis, d. Brathwait Massey——Henry Brower
——Nicholas Mitchell—— , wife of Goodwin.
1703-4—Thomas Ward——William Stevens, Sr.——
John Casey——Job Corking——Nicholas Hammer——Lidia,
w. Henry Dyer——Joseph Man——John Bartlett——Mary,
w. Ralph Hubard——Thos. Farmer, Jas. City Parish——
Mary, w. Joseph White——John Syncock——Edward, s.
Wm. Davis——John Wetherford——Mr. John Archer——
Robert West——Mr. Timothy Pinbethman.
1705—Frederick, s. Mr. Fred Jones——Sara, w. Capt.
Hugh Howell——William Cobbs——Mathew, s. Mr. James
and Mary Whaley——Denis, s. Flor. and Mary Mechart
——William Hopkins——Elizabeth, w. Edward Wigg——
Sidney Row——1706, Mary, w. John Ross——Robert
Filpott——1706, EDWARD NOTT, ESQ., GOV., Etc.——
Elizabeth Filpott, widow——John McCloud——John Hall.
1707—Mary, second w. Alexander Bonyman, clerk——
Thomas Pinchback——Richard Strickland——Wells, a very
ancient woman —— Anne Day —— Mr. Isaac Jemart,
Mercht.——Mrs. Minitrey, w. David Minitree——William
Gibbs, a very ancient man.
1708—Rebecca Pinkethman, widow——James Lord
——Nicholas Sebrill——Francis, w. Nicholas Sebrill——
Lucy, w. Jonathan Drewitt——Jane, w. Daniel Parke,
Esq.——Sara, w. John Nicolson——Cornelius Shehorne——
Catherine Masterson——Mrs. Lord, widow, James Lord.
1709—Mr. William Hansford——Mr. John Juce,
Keeper of prison——Mr. Thomas Wiggs.
1710—Godwin, w. William Thomas——Denis Shehorn
——Mary, d. Mr. Mengo Ingles——Elizabeth, d. Robert
Cobbs——Sarah, w. Henry Tyler——Hunphrey Hames
and wife——Mrs. Saml. Timson——Thomas Love——

Death Record

Joseph Bengerfield——Reinold Jackson, a very ancient man——Mr. Edward Powers——Mary, w. John Drewitt——John Leaver——Thomas Stanley——Jonathan Ratcliff——Joan, d. Widow Johnson——Thomas Hix——**The Reverend Mr. Solomon Whateley, Minister**——Rebecca, w Hen. Dyer——Mrs. Smith——Henry Dyer——Anne, d. Mungo Ingles——Mrs. Mouring, w. Capt. James Bray——Mrs. Francis Sharp.

1710-11 — Anne, w. Mungo Ingles —— Mary, w. Abraham Martin——Joseph White——William Pulley——Abraham Martin——Henry Gilbert——Edward Whittock——Mary, w. John Hall——Joseph, s. Francis Cook——1712, Mathew Lyndrick——Benjamin, s. Julius Cook——Sarah, d. Abraham Martin——Elizabeth, w. Wm. Alintof——Daughter of Fredk. Jones——Jane, d. Thomas Allen——Thomas Allen——David Minitree——Bentley.

1712—Mr. Coleman——Mr. William Pinkethman, High Sherr.——Mrs. Anne, d. Mr. Henry Tyler——Mr. Richard Wharton, Barister att Law——John Green——Anne, w. Mr. Thomas Read——Lydia, d. Robert Cobbe——John, Jr., s. Jno. Layton.

1713——Martin Denis——Frances, w. William Jones——Dorothy, w. Stephen Tomson——Elizabeth, d. Stephen Tomson, Esq.——Cobbs, d. Robert Cobbs.

1714—William Taylor——Anne, d. William and Mary Syms——John Timberleck——Issabella Broadbanck——John, s. John and Eliz. Tyler——William, s. Wm. and Mary Sherman——Elizabeth, w. Claud Rovear——Catherine, w. Harry Dyer —— Daughter of Eliz. Anderson —— David, s. John and Rachel Morris——William Lucas——Francis, w. John Custis——David, s Mungo Ingles——Elener, d. Thomas Wade.

1715—Mary, d. Alexander and Mary Gary——Son of John and Mary Hubbard——Christopher, s. Christopher and Mary Jackson——Sarah Dunston——Charles Barrett——John, s. David Stover (?)——Thomas, s. David and Eliz. Prior——Mary, d. William Davis.

1716—Mary, d. John and June Goodwin——Son of John and Mary Harris, (died unbaptized)——Sarah Dunston—— Johanna, d. Christ. and Mary Jackson——Dorcas, w. Samuel Timson —— 1717, Richard Davis —— George Glasscock——1718, William, s. James and Sarah Lewis—— John, s. John and Eliz. Bolton——John, s. Robert West—— Florence McCarty——Edward Dyer——1719, Danl., s. Danl. and Frances Burton——Hugh Norwell.

1719—Alexander Boniman——Florence, s. Florence McCarty——Daniel Blouette——Mary, w. Jno. Harris—— Mary Davis, widow——Rich. Huldston——Ambrose Cobbs Abigail Obrian——Matt Cole——Mary Baker——David Cunningham——Sarah, w. James Lewis——Mary Taylor ——Eliza, w. Francis Duffin.

1720—John Smith——Eliza, d. Georgee Riddal—— Child of Henry Cary——Bridgett Menetree, widow—— Barbary, d. Robert Laughton——William Cocke, Esq.—— Mrs. Judith Bray —— Joseph, s. Joseph and Eliza Davenport —— Peter Morgan —— Mr. Thos. Bray—— William, s. Sarah Taylor——Anne Moor——John Gooding ——Richard Williams——Alexander McGrigor——John Steward——Margett Bridson——Peter Owman——William Johnson.

1723—John Buffin——Taylor, s. Richard Tobin—— William, s. Frances Sharpe——Phileman Jackson—— Richard, s. Rich. and Mary Alcorn——John, s. Samuel and Eliz. Weldon——Thomas Tarrent——Hannah, d. William and Eliz. Rudder——Daniel Dean——George Gilbert——Ann Vaulx——Lydia, w. Wm. Dyer——Mary, d. Henry and Anne Cary.

1724—Daphne Lightfoot——Adam George——Benjamin Sadler——Alexander Kennedy——John West—— Jane, w. George Straghan——Joseph Davenport.

1725—Robert Fennock——Mr. Christian Munroe—— Thomas Paget——Charles Windsor——Lidia Dyer——John Pegram——Rachel Bakercet——Capt. James Bray—— Joanna Delony——Mr. Robert Cobb——James Cosby——

Margaret, w. Wm Alwood——William, s. John and Frances Ince——John Gill——**Mr. John Bag, Minister**—— 1726, Stephen Besouth——Thomas Wager——Thomas Harris——Jane Newman——Sarah, w. George Straugham ——1727, Mary Pasteur——James Backhurst——Thomas Barber —— Jane Ogleby —— John Davis, Sen.——Jno. Pasteur, Sen. s. Jno. Pasteur——James Shields—— **Edmund Jennings, Esq.**——Eliza Pack——Mrs. Mary Luke —— William Harrison —— Elizabeth, w. Joseph Davenport—— William Johnsoune—— William, s. Wm. Bulger——Sanders, w. Robert Sanders.

1726—Eliza Wilkinson——Ann, w. John Davenport—— Ann Everitt——Wm. Allexander——Andrew, s. Andrew Laprade——Ann, w. Andrew Laprade——Peter Serjeanten ——Michale Archer——Mary Lark——Mary Green—— Elizabeth Archer——William Forbar——Jno., son John Pasteur——Eliza Willis——Mary Kains——Hannah Bryan ——Jean Pollard——Eliza Wilkinson——Daniel Taylor—— Daniel Murpha——John Davis, Jr.——Samuel Millington ——Frances Millington——Wm. Humphreys——William Barber —— Benjamin Stone —— William, s. John and Hannah Whitehead——Mary Nicholas——John Harris.

1728—William Dyer——Mrs. Sarah Jennings, widow of Col. Edward Jennings, Pres.——John Davis——Anne, d. John and Eliza Tyler——Martha, d. Robert Dyer—— Edward, Child Edward Burrish——Margaret Thompson ——Frances Young——Elizabeth, d. Wm. and Francis Aleraft.

1729—Mr. Giles Moodey —— Bettey Jacquelin, d. Richard Pack——William, s. Capt. James Hopkins—— Amy, w. Charles Cosby——Elizabeth, d. Henry Bryan—— William Thompson——Daniel LeMerchant——Elizabeth, d. Susane Cooper——Sara, w. Isaac Bee——Itilla, d. James and Mary Hubard——Lewis Contesse——Margaret, w. John White——Patrick Green——John Brook——George Wynn——Mr. Henry Tyler, Sen.——Ann, widow John Davis ——William Stone——Sarah, d. John Pa—— ——

1734—Garret Henrikiss——John, s. John Lang——Rachael Wood——John Cook——Thomas Rogerman——Elizabeth Newton——Thomas Couser——William Harper.
1735—Jane, w. Dennis Barden——Catherine Moreland——Mrs. Elizabeth, w. John Timson——Helena, w. William Maples——Robert Johnson——Daniel Cain——William, s. William Trewly——Anthony Hammond——Sarah, d. Jno. Blair——James, s. John Mundell——Ann, d. Henry Tyler.
1736—Elizabeth Johnson, widow —— Mr. William Blaikley —— Mary, d. Mrs. Charles Bridges, Sr. —— Elizabeth, w. Saml. Pennele——Hugh Edmunds——John Douglass——Mr. Henry Skipwith——Mrs. Skaif, w. Rev. John Skaif, Rector of Stratton (?) —— ——
1737—William Hunt——Jeky C. Jones——Anne, d. Anne Jorgles——Mary, w. William Taylor——Daughter of Gabriel Maupin——Catherine Oconnor——John Clayton, Esq.——Sarah Bryum——Elizabeth, w. James Shields——Rebecca, d. Thomas and Eliza Penman——William Burum——Mary, d. James Spence——Hon. William Gooch, Esq.——Major Abraham Nicholas——Mr. Alexander Kerr——Rachael Rhodewell——Sary, d. Sarah Roadwell——Dennis Folio——Eliza, d. Wm. and Eliza Wyatt——Judith, d. Gabriel Maupin——John, s. in law Philip Hankins——John Macgrigor——Patrick Fergusson.
1748—Elizabeth, d. John Holt, Merchant——Mary, d. Doctor Kenneth McKensie——Thomas Prat——Elizabeth Fleming——John, s. John Holt, Merchant——Mrs. Crease, w. Thos. Crease——Thos , s. George Camp——Elizabeth, w. James Levie——Richard Stannup——William Ninimo or Nimmo, Esq.——Hannah, d. James Wray, d. Jas. Wray, Esq.——Anne Stevens——Elizabeth, d. Philip Jackson——Charles Lewis——Elizabeth, d. William Timson——James Reynolds——William Buck——Hon. John Groymes——Mrs. Sarah, w. Mr Henry Tyler —— Mr. John Stott, Watchmaker——William Parris——Sarah Pegram——John Leppers——James Colvil——Ralph Graves——Mrs. John

Death Record

Rawley——Sarah Lynne——Mrs. Wm. Timson——George Charlton Taylor——Mr. Davidson——Mrs. Davidson——John Custis, Esq.

1751—Abraham, s. Abrm. Nicholas and Anne——1761, Mr. Abraham Nicholas, Sen,, Clerk of the Church.

Historical Addenda

SUBSEQUENT to printing the preceding part of this book, the following historical notes have come to light, and are inserted here for preservation, and because of their historic interest.

In an article on the "Church at Jamestown" in the Church Review of April, 1855, we have found four verbal extracts from the Bruton Parish Vestry Book of 1674 which are not included in the extracts from this old Vestry Book hitherto given. Two of these are in connection with a dispute as to

The Boundary Line Between James City Parish and Bruton Parish.

Under date the 8th of May, 1691, there was the following record:

"Whereas we are informed that some persons of JAMES CITTY PARISH have a design to deprive THIS parish of their undoubted right, endeavoring by the present General Assembly to augment THEIR parish, by lessening OURS, it is therefore the order and request of this present Vestry, that Mr. Samuel Eburne [Minister,] Cap't. Francis Page, Mr. Edmund Jenings, Mr. Martin Gardner, Mr. Saml. Simson, and Mr. John Ownes, doe appear before ye Governor and Councill and Burgesses of this present Generall Assembly, to make out how this parish hath been established by as good authority as Virginia can give,—That our parish remain entire as settled by former Assemblys, ffor we cannot think that this assembly will take away any man's property without his consent, and to do that from a Corporation or Parish, which may not be done to a single person, is a greater injury:—And therefore we have good reason to think that the General Assembly will rather rattify our just right and property which we have quietly enjoyed time out of mind, than any ways infringe the same."

Parish Processioned

At this same meeting of the Vestry of the 8th of May, 1691, it was also determined that,

"Whereas it is thought convenient by this Vestry for preventing OTHER PARISHES making encroachments upon the bounds of ours, that the bounds of our Parish be surrounded by ye inhabitants, and processioned. It is therefore ordered that the Vestry do meet ye first Thursday in December next, to consult of such method as may be thought most convenient ffor effecting ye same; and that in ye meantime ye present Church Wardens make what inquiry they can of ye bounds of that part of the Parish which bounds on James Cittie Parish."

Size of Doors in Church at James City and Bruton

In the record of the proceedings of the Vestry of Bruton Parish, held on June 5th, 1679, among other items relating to building the new Church at Middle Plantation (Williamsburg), it is required that,

"Ye West door and Chancell door be according to the dimensions of James City Church door, only to be one foot higher and ½ a foot wider than they are."

Mr. Francis Durfey Ordered to His Home Parish

In 1725 it is recorded in the Vestry Book of Bruton Parish that,—

"Whereas Francis Durfey hath this day (December 17th,) made application for relief from this Vestry, but it appearing that he is a lawful resident of James City Parish, Ordered, that he forthwith remove out of this Parish."

The Removal and Restoration of the Jamestown Communion Silver

At the Convention of the Diocese of Virginia, held in Lynchburg in May, 1854, the Revd. John Grammar presented the Jamestown Communion Silver to the Convention with the following statement:

"I beg leave to state to this Convention, that I have set upon the table three pieces of communion plate which originally belonged to the Church of Jamestown, the first Protestant Episcopal Church that was planted on the American continent. This plate was under the care of the Vestry of Bruton Parish, Williamsburg, when the Jamestown Church fell into disuse, and became extinct. In the summer of 1827, when I was about to be ordained a Presbyter, the Vestry of that Parish learning through the Revd. Dr. Wilmer, who was then Rector, that the Parishes in which I was ministering, and endeavoring to revive and re-organize, were destitute of communion plate, very kindly and most unexpectedly sent me these three pieces, accompanied by a resolution requiring me to preserve the same, and to return to said Vestry an acknowledgment of its receipt, and an obligation binding myself in the contingency of the future resuscitation of the Church in the old Jamestown Island, and the Canonical Organization of a Parish therein in connection with the Protestant Episcopal Church in the Diocese of Virginia, to restore the said plate to such Church. Such acknowledgment and obligation I accordingly forthwith forwarded to the said Vestry, and from that time have kept the said plate under my own custody, having used it only on the first occasion of my administration of the Sacrament of the Lord's Supper, when finding the size of the Chalice rendered its use inconvenient, and being otherwise provided with more convenient plate, this has since remained in disuse. These three pieces comprise a large Silver Chalice, inscribed on the side,

"Mixe not Holy Thinges with Profane;"

and under the foot the words

"Ex dono Francisci Morrison Armigeri, A. D. 1661."

A Silver Patten with the same words inscribed on its bottom and underneath its foot, and a Silver Alms basin or plate, having inscribed on its rim the words,

"For the use of James City Parish Church."

Having occasion some few years since to make inquiry, I learned from the Rev. H. M. Dennison, then Rector of Bruton Parish, that my obligation to the Vestry above mentioned could not be found, and that no record of the proceedings of the Vestry of Bruton Parish for 1827, and several succeeding years, had been preserved;[1] and the knowledge of this fact suggesting to me the impropriety of having property over which the Convention only can be regarded as having any rightful ownership, in irresponsible and consequently insecure hands, I have brought the said plate with me to this place, and now present it to the Convention with the suggestion and request that it be committed to —— ——, to be deposited by them in the Library of the Theological Seminary of Virginia, there to be carefully preserved as a valuable historical memorial of our fathers, by whose pious zeal the Church of our affections was first planted in our land."

On motion it was

"Resolved, That the Communion plate surrendered to this Convention by the Rev. John Grammar, be now committed to the charge of the Rev. Drs. Sparrow and Packard, to be by them carried to the Theological Seminary, and deposited in the Library thereof, to be there carefully preserved."[2]

---

[1] The Vestry Book opens with record of meeting held May, 1827.
[2] Virginia Convention Journal, 1854, pp. 35, 36.

Returned to Bruton Parish

In the minutes of the Convention of the Diocese of Virginia, held in 1858, we find the following record:

"Mr. Barton presented a memorial from the Vestry of Bruton Parish, praying the restoration to their possession and care of certain plate which once belonged to the Church at Jamestown, but which by an order of the Convention of 1854, was deposited for safe keeping in the Library of the Theological Seminary, near Alexandria. The said memorial, on motion, was referred to a committee, consisting of Mr. D. W. Barton (Winchester), Rev. William N. Pendleton, and Mr. David H. Conrad (Norborne Parish, Berkley Co.)[1]

On page 41 of this Journal of 1858 we find the following:

"The Committee to whom was referred the memorial of Bruton Parish, with regard to the plate formerly belonging to the Church at Jamestown, now in the Library of the Theological Seminary, presented their report, and on motion it was recommitted to the Committee, to lie over until the next meeting of the Convention."

This Committee reported to the Convention of 1859, which was attended by Rev. G. T. Wilmer and Dr. Robert M. Garrett from Bruton Parish. The record is in the following words:

"The Committee of the last Convention on the memorial of Bruton Parish, praying that the plate formerly belonging to the Church at Jamestown, and now in the Library of the Virginia Theological Seminary, may be restored to the vestry of the said (Bruton) Parish, reported that they had no further information to communicate, and renewed the recommendation that the prayer of the memorialists be granted."

"The report was adopted."[2]

---

[1] Virginia Convention Journal, 1858, p. 37.
[2] Virginia Convention Journal, 1859, p. 42.

These Convention records have been copied to give answer to the question, which is often asked, as to the right and authority by which Bruton Church holds this silver, which this Parish Church, as the successor of the Church at Jamestown, inherited in 1699, or after the Jamestown Church was burned in 1676, during Bacon's rebellion.

Inscription on the Custis' Tombs

On the outside of Bruton Church, in the corner where the north wall intersects the north wing at the west, next to the tomb of Col. Daniel Parke, are two tombs removed, with the remains of the persons they commemorate, from *New Kent Co.*, Virginia. They are inscribed,—

>Here lies the body of
>Mrs. Frances Custis
>daughter of Daniel Park Esq.,
>who departed this life
>March the 14th, 17$\frac{14}{15}$ in the 29th
>year of Her Age.

>Here lies the body of
>Daniel Park Custis
>son of Col. Daniel Park Custis
>of New Kent County
>who Departed this Life
>on the 19th of February, 1754
>Aged two years and three months.

>Under this stone lies interred
>the body of Frances Park
>Custis daughter of Daniel
>Park Custis, Esqr., and Martha*
>his wife born April 12th 1753,
>Dyed April 1st 1757
>—— 4 years.

---

*Subsequently Mrs. Martha Washington.

Scattered Tomb-stones

Scattered through James City, and the counties adjacent, are a large number of old tomb-stones, many of which mark the graves of persons whose names are well known in the history of Virginia. Many of these grave yards are being sold to immigrants as parts of purchased farms. In some instances, at least, the tomb-stones will be regarded as being in the way. The stones will be removed and used in building, the ground will be left unmarked, and pass into cultivation. The Drummond tomb-stone at Green Spring, the former residence of Sir William Berkley, three miles from Jamestown, was for years used as a floor in a spring house, and then placed in a cart to be carried to the house for a door step, and, on being dumped from the cart, was broken in two, and now lies out in the yard. These stones could be preserved, and the dust of the departed dead would be protected from desecration if the tomb-stones and the remains of the dead could be removed from these neglected and abandoned farms and placed for preservation and protection in the yard of Bruton Parish Church, or in the Church itself. This was done in the case of the Custis tombs, from which the inscriptions given above were taken. Since this idea has been suggested others have taken steps looking to the removal of the tombs of their ancestors from neglected farms to these hallowed grounds.

A diagram will be prepared and preserved, showing the exact location of the tombs now in the Church and Church yard, and of others placed there. This, with the record of inscriptions given in this book, will insure the permanent location of these tombs even after the effacing touch of time shall have made the inscriptions in the marble illegible. The location and the inscriptions of the tombs will thus be preserved as a part of the historical record of this historic Church and place.

Introductory Note

Relating to the Baptism of Slaves

In the old Parish Register of 1662 we find thirty-three consecutive pages devoted entirely to the record of the baptism of slaves, or colored servants. This record extends from 1746 to 1797. The record of the baptisms has, however, been preserved for only twenty-five years during this period. A number of pages were torn from the book and used, it is said, for wrapping preserve jars. The book was found at the home of Mrs. McCandlish, and given into the custody of the late Dr. Coleman. There appears no record for the following years, inclusive—*i. e.*, from 1755 to 1758, from 1769 to 1781, from 1784 to 1787, and from 1792 to 1796, making twenty-six years of which there are no records under the heading of the Baptism of Slaves.

The following summary shows the number of slaves baptized each year of which there is record, and the total number baptized for each person whose name is given during the years designated, inclusive.

While we have no desire to defend slavery as an institution, and with no intention of doing so, we point with a feeling of commendable gratification to the fact that our representative southern people were earnestly solicitous as to the spiritual care of these colored people. To this fact this record is a witness. And as an abiding witness to this truth it has been compiled and inserted. The number of colored people baptized in Bruton Parish in the year 1750 was larger by one than the total number of infant and adult baptisms of colored people by our Church in the whole Diocese of Southern Virginia as reported to the Council in 1903.

A successful work was conducted among the colored people by the Revd. Wm. Hodges, D. D., 1837-1848. There

Introductory Note Relating to Baptism of Slaves

are no records extant showing the results of this undertaking. A mission for colored people has recently been organized in the Parish, and is now being conducted under the direction of the rector.

W. A. R. G.

BRUTON PARISH HOUSE,
February 1, 1904.

The Number of Slaves Baptized in Bruton Parish Each Year for Twenty-five Years

1746	8	1764	65
1747	40	1765	75
1748	29	1766	94
1749	54	1767	78
1750	116	1768	87
1751	73	1782	32
1752	33	1783	69
1753	28	1788	1
1754	69	1790	1
1759	2	1791	1
1760	2	1797	1
1761	25	Free Slaves baptized from 1746	
1762	66	to 1797	37
1763	36		

Total number baptized, ...1122

Alphabetical List of Persons who had Slaves Baptized

with the number baptized for each person named, during the years, inclusive, designated—
See Introductory Note, page 152

Name of Owner	No. Slaves Baptized
Ambler, Richard, 1751,	1
Amy, Mrs., 1761,	1
Anderson, Andrew, 1750,	1
Anderson, Robert, 1782-'83,	2
Anson, Doctor, 1750-'04,	2
Armistead, Booth, 1752,	2
Armistead, Elyson, 1750-02,	2
Armistead, Robert, 1762,	1
Attorney, the, 1747,	1
Ayescough, Christopher, 1768,	1
Baker, Jonathan, 1765-'67,	2
Barber, the Widow, 1749-'50,	4
Bardett, 1754,	1
Barradall, Mrs., 1754,	5
Baskerfield, 1750,	2
Basset, Mrs. and widow, 1749-'68,	4
Bates, James, 1748,	1
Beall, Saml., 1782-'83,	3
Bellini, Chas., 1783,	1
Besser, Jno. S., 1743,	1
Blaikley, Mrs., 1748,	1
Blaikley, Katharine, 1765-'67,	1
Blair, Hon. Col. Jno., Esq., 1747-'82.	24
Bocock, Mrs., 1754,	1
Bowcock, Edw., 1750-'51,	2
Booker, Richard, 1783,	2
Bray, Coll. Thos., 1747-51,	14
Bray, Maj., 1750-'54,	6
Bray, widow, 1750,	6
Brown, John, 1753-'66,	3
Brown, Wm., 1752-'64,	2
Bruton Parish,	1
Bryan, Benj., 1749-'51,	4

Name of Owner	No. Slaves Baptized
Bryan, Fredk., 1762-'68,	16
Bryan, Estate Fredk., 1782,	2
Bryan, John, 1747-'83,	4
Bryan, Mary, 1762,	1
Bryan, Widow, 1751,	1
Bryan, William, 1754,	1
Buford, Mr., 1754,	2
Bullifant, Phillip, 1767-'82,	2
Burdett, Mrs. Kitty, 1748,	1
Burfoot, Lawson, 1752-65,	4
Burwell, Armistead, 1747,	1
Burwell, Bacon, Est., 1749,	1
Burwell, Col. Carter, 1749-'54,	23
Burwell, Col. Carter, Est., 1762-'68,	18
Burwell, James, 1766,	1
Burwell, Col. Lewis, 1747-'68,	70
Burwell, Widow, 1761,	1
Camp, Geo., 1752,	1
Camp, Jno. 1763-'68,	5
Camp, Mary, 1763,	1
Camp, Mrs., 1754,	1
Campbell, Mary, 1765,	2
Campbell, Jno., 1761,	1
Campbell, Katharine, 1762-'67,	5
Campbell, Widow, 1753,	1
Carter, Jas., 1765,	1
Carter, John, 1759-1788,	3
Carter, Coll. Landon, 1747-1767,	14
Carter, Coll. Landon, Est., 1761,	1
Carter, Hon. Robt., 1761-'68,	12
Carter, William, 1768,	1
Carter, Mrs., 1754,	1

Alphabetical List of Persons who had Slaves Baptized

Name of Owner	No. Slaves Baptized
Chapman, John, 1768,	1
Charlton, Edwd., 1752-'68,	4
Charlton, Mrs., 1751,	1
Chiswell, Coll. Jno., 1752-'66,	5
Chiswell, Mrs.,	2
Chowning, Josiah, 1666'-67,	2
Coales, Thos., 1783,	1
Cobbs, Mrs. Mary, 1751-'67,	5
Cobbs, Thomas, 1750-'67,	2
Cocke, James, 1764-'68	3
Coke, James, 1762,	1
Coke, John, 1748-'82,	2
Coke, Saml, 1762,	1
Coke, Thomas, 1750,	1
College, See Wm. and Mary,	
Cosby, Mark, 1747-'49,	2
Cotton, Mrs. Lucy, 1749-'64,	2
Coulthard, Wm., 1754,	1
Craige, James, 1764,	1
Craige, Alex., 1765-'68,	6
Crawley, John, 1783,	3
Crawley, Natthaniel, 1750-'67,	12
Crawley, Robert, 1753,	1
Crawley, Robert, Est., 1768,	2
Crawley, Samuel, 1782.	2
Crawley, Widow, 1752,	1
Crease, Mrs. 1754,	2
Custis, Coll. Daniel, 1750-'64,	6
Custis, Coll. John, 1747-'65,	7
Custis, Col. 1747-'66,	16
Custis, Col, Estate, 1765-'68,	9
Dale, Lidder, 1750,	1
Davenport, George, 1750-'66,	5
Davenport, Joseph, 1750-'51,	2
Davenport, Martha, 1764-'67,	2
Dawson, Revd. Commissary, 1747-'50,	3
Dawson, Elizabeth, 1762-'68,	3
Dawson, Priscilla, 1762-'67,	4
Dawson, Widow, 1752-'65,	2
Day, Benj., 1783,	1
Dickenson, Thos., 1750,	1
Dickenson, John, 1766,	1

Name of Owner	No. Slaves Baptized
Dickinson, Arthur, 1765,	1
Digges, Dudley, 1783,	1
Dixon, Doctor, 1748-'51,	4
Dixon, John, 1768-'83,	2
Dixon, Widow, 1747,	1
Druitz, J. C., 1783,	1
Drumond, Mrs. Amey, 1766-'68,	3
Drumond, Mrs. Amey, Est., 1783,	1
Eaton, Mary, 1762-64,	5
Eaton, Penkethman, 1751,	3
Eaton, William, 1766-'83,	3
English, Mary, 1764,	1
Everard, Thomas, 1749-'68,	15
Fauquier, Hon. Francis, Gov., 1762-'67,	4
Fergusson, Colins, 1762-'65,	2
Fergusson, John, 1762-'68,	5
Finnie, Alex., 1749, '67,	4
Finnie, Leander, 1764,	1
Finnie, William, 1764-'82,	4
Free Slaves, 1746-'97,	37
Galt, James, 1766-'83,	7
Garland, John, 1767,	1
Garland, Widow, 1767,	2
Geddy, 1766,	1
Gilbert, Peter, 1751-'83,	2
Gilmer (or more,) Dr. Geo., 1749-'65,	11
Glass, 1762,	1
Gooch, Hon. Wm.. Gov., 1750-'54,	5
Goodson, Mr., Estate, 1783,	1
Gough, Mrs., 1749,	1
Graves, Chas., 1783,	1
Graves, Ralph, 1747,	1
Graves, William, 1762-'68,	7
Green, Mr., 1783,	1
Greenhow, John, 1762-'64,	2
Griffin, Dr. Cyrus, 1783,	1
Grymes, Mary, 1764-'66,	4
Gun, Mr., 1783,	

156 Alphabetical List of Persons who had Slaves Baptized

Name of Owner	No. Slaves Baptized
Hansford, Edward, 1763,	2
Hansford, Thomas, 1763,	1
Hansford, Mrs., 1750,	1
Harmer, Mrs., 1750,	1
Harwood, Humphrey, 1768-'82,	2
Hay, Anthony, 1759-'68,	5
Hay, Dr. Peter, 1766,	2
Holloway, Mrs., 1747-'54,	2
Holt, John, 1748-'50,	2
Holt, Thomas, 1762,	1
Holt, William, 1764-'67,	8
Hornsby, Thomas, 1748-'68,	8
Hornsby, William, 1783,	1
Horrocks, Rev'd James, 1767-'68,	2
Hubard, Morton, 1782,	1
Hubard, William, 1748-'68,	3
Hubard, Mrs., 1748-'83,	4
Hubbard, Mrs., 1754,	3
Hughs, Emery, 1763-'82,	2
Hughes, Jas., 1782-'83,	2
Hulett, Hannah, 1768-'83,	2
Jackson, Geo., 1783,	5
Jackson, Phips., 1751-'52,	2
Jackson, Sarah, 1761,	2
Jameson, David, 1767,	1
Johnson, Coll. Phillip, 1751-'68,	29
Jones, Coll. Thos., 1747-'54,	3
Keele, Mrs., 1754,	1
Keith, Mrs., 1750,	1
Kemp, Rebecca, 1783,	1
Kendall, Jno., 1747,	1
Kene, Mrs., 1750,	2
Kennedy, William, 1754,	2
Larke, Robt., 1761,	1
Lane, John, 1752,	1
Lawson, Saml., 1765,	1
Lewis, John, 1782,	1
Long, David, 1751,	1
Lyne, Betty, 1751,	1
Major, Saml., 1782-'83,	2
Maupin, Gabriel, 1764-'83,	3
Maupin, Mrs., 1750-'54,	2
May, Peter, 1763,	1
Maynard, Edward, 1751-'53,	2
McCarty, Elizabeth, 1747,	1
McCarty, James, 1767,	2
McCarty, John, 1747,	2
McCarty, Michael, 1762,	1
McClurg, Dr., 1783,	1
McKenzie, Dr. Kenneth, 1749-'54,	7
Metcalf, Matthew, 1751,	1
Moody, Matthew, 1748-'64,	4
Moody, Martha, 1766,	1
Moody, Phillip, 1768,	1
Moody, William, 1764-'83,	4
Morton, David, 1782,	1
Moss, William, 1762-'68,	3
Moyer, Peter, 1765, '82,	2
Mundell, Mr., 1754,	1
Nelson, General, 1783,	3
Nicholas, Robert Carter, 1753-'64,	8
Nicholson, Edw., Est., 1768.	1
Nicholson, Rob't, 1766-'97,	8
Nicholson, William, 1782,	1
Newitt, Richard, 1762,	1
Newitt, William, 1762,	1
Orr, Mr., 1782,	1
Page, John, 1752,	1
Page, Mary, 1762-'67,	2
Palmer, John, 1749,	1
Paradice, Estate, 1782,	1
Parker, Mr., 1754,	1
Parks, William, 1750,	1
Parrott, Jos., Estate, 1766,	1
Pastuer, William, 1763-'66,	2
Patterson, Mrs., 1747-'54,	2
Peale, John, 1751,	1
Pearson, Matthew, 1783,	1
Penny, Penl. 1782,	1
Peters, Anthony, 1751,	1
Pierce, Matthew, 1747-'68,	7
Pitt, George, 1762-'67,	9
Potter, Dr., 1754,	1
Powell, Benj., 1762-'83,	8

Alphabetical List of Persons who had Slaves Baptized

Name of Owner	No. Slaves Baptized
Prentis, Eliz., 1768,	1
Prentis, Joseph, 1782-'83,	2
Prentis, Mary, 1768,	1
Prentis, William, 1748-'67,	13
Priar, Fredk., 1762,	1
Purdy, Alex., 1765-'67,	3
Randal, Attorney, 1749,	1
Randal, Lady, 1754,	2
Randolph, John, 1763-'68,	5
Randolph, Peyton, 1748-'68,	17
Randolph, Lady, 1750,	2
Ratcliff, William, 1751,	1
Reid, George, 1782,	1
Riddel, Mrs , 1783,	1
Roadman, Mr., 1783,	1
Roberts, Abe, 1747,	1
Roberts, William, 1768,	1
Robinson, Revd. Thos., 1749-'53,	2
Royle, Joseph, 1762-'64,	2
Royle, Joseph. *Est.*, 1766,	1
Royle, Mrs., 1766,	1
Russel, John, 1749,	1
Russel, William, 1783,	1
Saunders, John, 1761-'83,	5
Saunders, William, 1764,	1
Scarborough, Col., 1747-'50,	2
Scarborough, Mrs., 1749-'54,	5
Shields, James, 1747-'83,	31
Shields, Matthew, 1747-'56,	3
Shoemaker, Jas. Taylor, 1766-68,	2
Short, Widow, 1752,	1
Sidderdel, Mrs., 1750,	3
Singleton, Ann, 1762,	1
Singleton, Ann, Est., 1765-'66,	2
Smith, Capt., 1754,	1
Southall, Francis, 1763,	1
Southall, James, 1765-'83,	5
Spratley, William, 1751-'53,	2
Spurr, Saml., 1762-'68,	6
Stark, Richard, 1767-'68,	2
Stay, Anthony, 1762,	1
Steel, Mary, 1747-'64,	6
Stevinson, Mr., 1749,	1
Stith, Judith, 1766-'68,	2
Stith, Mary, 1751-'68,	4
Stith, President Wm., 1753,	2
Stott, Mr. 1754,	2
Street, Richard, 1767,	2
Swiney, Major, 1748,	1
Taliaferro, Charles, 1783,	1
Tarpley, Edward, 1749-'50,	3
Tarpley, Mrs. Eliz., 1748-'66,	6
Taylor, James, 1763,	1
Taylor, John, 1748-'54,	3
Thornton, William, 1763,	1
Timson, William, 1749-'50,	5
Timson, S., Estate, 1782,	1
Timson, Widow,	2
Trebell, William, 1760-'68,	1
Turner, Joseph, 1750,	1
Tyler, Henry, 1750,	1
Valentine, Joseph, 1765-'82,	2
Vobe, Jane, 1762-'68,	4
Waller, Benjamin, 1746-'82,	39
Walters, Wm., 1764-'66,	2
Washington, Coll. George, 1762-68,	11
Warters, Wm., 1762-'65,	2
Weatherburn, Ann, 1764,	1
Weatherburn, Henry, 1749-'62,	1
Weatherburn Estate,	1
Wheatly, John, 1751,	1
Whitaker, Simon, 1764-'65,	2
Wm. and Mary College 1749-'83,	21
Willis, Coll. Francis, 1782-'68,	20
Woody, Matthew, 1752,	1
Wray, James, 1747-'83,	12
Wray, Mary, 1751-'67,	3
Wythe, George, 1781-'83,	2
Wythe, Nathaniel, Decd., 1760,	1
Yates, Revd. Wm., 1762-'64,	4
Total,	1122

Alphabetical List of Communicants of Bruton Church from 1868 to 1904

NOTE—This list is as complete as it has been possible to make it. All the names inscribed in the Parish register from 1868 to 1904 are given. Where no records were made, as frequently was the case, an effort has been made to procure supplementary data. The names are given as they were entered, and there are many who are therefore recorded under their maiden name. The date indicates the time when the name was entered, or should have been entered.

* Present Communicants. † Name after marriage. †† Maiden name.

*Alexander, Mrs. Ann Letitia 1903
Ambler, Mrs. Thos. M., 1868,
Anderson, Mrs., 1868,
*Armistead, Miss Julia Champion, 1891,
Armistead, Miss Mary, (M. Holt†) 1879,
Armistead, Mrs. Rebecca H., 1894
*Armistead, Mr. Robt., 1870,
*Armistead, Mrs. Robt., 1870,
Armistead, Miss Virginia Travis (M. Hardy†), 1891,
Armistead, Mrs. Virginia Edwards, 1891,
Barrett, Mr. Chas., 1889,
*Becker, Mr. H. S., 1901,
Bibb, Wm. L., (Student) 1891,
*Bird, Prof. Hugh S., 1903,
*Bird, Mrs. Hugh (Smith†), 1903,
Bishop, Mrs. Chas. Edw., 1892,
*Bloxton, Miss Lucy, 1895,
*Bloxton, Miss Letitia W., 1903,
Bloxton, Miss Mary Coleman, 1895,
*Booth, Miss Clara T., 1900,
*Booth, Dr. E. G., 1887,
†Booth, Mrs. E. G., 1887,
Booth, Miss Frances R., (M. Ballentine†), 1892,

Booth, Miss Henrietta E. (M. Wise†), 1894,
Booth, Miss Lucy (M. Cumming†), 1887,
*Booth, Thompson, 1903,
Bowery, Chas. Bushrod, 1891,
*Bowery, Miss Imogene, 1900,
Bowman, Mr. Sherrard, 1871,
Bowman, Mrs. Sherrard, 1871,
Boyden, Mr. P. M., 1870,
*Braithwaite, Mrs. Delia A., 1869,
Braithwaite, Miss Louise (M. Long†), 1900,
*Braithwaite, Miss Minnie G., 1890
*Braithwaite, Miss Ruth, 1900,
*Braithwaite, Miss Virginia, 1901,
Braithwaite, Wm., 1885,
*Braithwaite, W. H., 1887,
Branch, Mrs. Cyrus A., 1868,
Branch, Matilda, 1885,
Bright, Mrs. Elizabeth, 1868,
*Bright, Miss Jean (M. Mercer†), 1868,
Bright, Miss Nannie (M. Cook†)
*Bright, Capt. Robt. A., 1871,
Bright, Mrs. Robt. A., 1871,
Bright, Robt. A., Jr., 1884,
*Brooks, Miss Cora (M. Johnson†), 1887,

List of Communicants from 1868 to 1904   159

*Brooks, Mrs. Margaret, 1887,
*Brooks, Wm. Montague, 1893,
Brower, Dr. D. R., 1871,
Brower, Mrs., 1871,
Brown, Anne Chiswell, 1869,
Brown, Miss Sue, 1884,
Brownell, Mrs., 1868,
*Bucktrout, Mrs. Horatio, 1893,
Burke, Chas. W., 1893,
Burke, Francis M., 1891,
Burke, Mrs. Maria (Charles††) 1891,
Burke, Thomas Michael, 1891,
*Burns, Miss Clara (M. Brooks) 1899,
Burrows, Harry L. (Student), 1904,
Buskey, Jas. G. (Student), 1892,
Camm, Miss Annie, 1871,
Camm, Charlie, 1884,
Camm, Dr. Edward, 1869,
Camm, Mrs. Edward, 1869,
Camm, Edward, Jr., 1869,
Camm, Miss Florence, 1870,
Camm, Frank, 1869,
Camm, John, 1871,
Cary, Miss Harriett (M. Christian†), 1868,
Cary, Mrs. Lucy N., 1868,
Chichester, Jno. C. (Student), 1892
*Christian, Miss Emily, 1887,
Christian, Hodges M., 1893,
*Christian, Mr. James T., 1887,
Christian, Marston, 1895,
Christian, Wm. T., 1891,
*Christian, Mrs. Wm. T., 1884,
Claiborne, Mrs. Mary B., 1868,
Claiborne, Randolph, R. (Student), 1892,
Clopton, Miss Charlotte, 1887,
Clopton, Dr. John, 1868,
Clopton, Miss Kate, 1887,
Clowes, E. H., 1887,
*Cocke, Miss Julia, 1884,

*Cole, Henry Dennison, 1903,
Cole, Mr. R. F., 1870,
Cole, Mrs. Robt. F., 1868,
Cole, Robt. R., 1871,
Cole, Edward, 1871,
Coleman, Dr. Chas. W., 1868,
*Coleman, Mrs. Chas. W., 1868,
Coleman, C. W. J., 1884,
*Coleman, Miss Elizabeth, 1884,
*Coleman, Miss Helen (M. Leigh†), 1868,
Coleman, George Preston, 1887,
Coleman, Tucker, 1884,
*Colonna, Wm. E. (Student), 1903
Cosnahan, Hugh Mercer, 1872,
*Cosnahan, Miss Mary M. (M. Stubbs†), 1868,
Cosnahan, Miss Roberta O. (M. Camm†), 1868,
Coupland, Mr. John, 1871,
Coupland, Mrs. John, 1868,
*Coupland, Miss Julia (M. Hundley†), 1868,
*Coupland, Miss Nora (M. Spencer†), 1871,
Coupland, Robert, 1887,
Custis, Mrs. Clara, 1868,
*Custis, Miss Elizabeth F. (M. Ambler†), 1871,
Custis, Miss Kate, 1869,
Custis, Miss Florence (M. Cole†), 1869,
*Custis, Miss Margaret (M. Hansford†), 1869,
Cutherell, Mr., 1871,
Cutherell, Mrs., 1871,
Darlington, Mrs., 1868,
*Darlington, Miss Mary (M. Jones†), 1871,
Darlington, Miss Kate (M. Johnson†), 1868,
Davis, Mrs., 1868,
Davis, Miss Lucy Lee, (?) 1897,
*Davis, Miss Nannie, 1903,

List of Communicants from 1868 to 1904

Day, Chas. Fenton, 1890,
Dix, Mrs. Sarah, 1868,
Dixon, Miss Betty (M. Morrison†), 1868,
Dixon, C. C., 1884,
Dod, Mr. Chas. S., 1871,
Dod, Mrs. Chas. S., 1871,
Dodgson, Miss, 1870,
Durfey, Coll. G., 1868,
*Durfey, Mr. Z. G., 1902,
Edloe, Miss Sally B., 1868,
Edwards, Mr. Thomas G., 1871,
Eldred, Mrs. Harriett A., 1893,
*Elwood, Mr. Michael, 1903,
Evans, Mrs. Julia U., 1868,
Ewell, Coll. Benj. S., 1868,
*Falkiner, Miss Charlotte (M. Hubbard†), 1883,
*Falkiner, Miss Ida, 1887,
*Foster, Dr. Littleberry S., 1903,
*Foster, Mrs. L. S., 1899,
*Foster, Miss Lucile, 1903,
*Foster, Miss Mary, 1899,
*Foster, W. Dixon, 1903,
*Galt, Miss Annie A., 1893,
Galt, Miss Elizabeth A., 1899,
Galt, Miss Mary J., 1894,
Galt, Miss Mary M., 1897,
Galt, Mrs. Mary W., 1893,
Galt, Miss Sally M., 1868,
*Garrett, Miss Lottie, 1868,
*Garrett, Miss Mary, 1871,
Garrett, Dr. Robt. M., 1868,
Garrett, Mrs. Robt. M., 1868,
Garrett, Miss Susan C. (M. Nelson†), 1871,
*Garrett, Dr. Van F., 1869,
*Garrett, Mrs. Van F., 1896,
Garrett, W. R., 1868,
Gay, Miss Bettie, 1871,
Glover, Perkins (Student), 1891,
*Goodwin, Mrs. W. A. R., 1903,
*Gore, Mr. Wm., 1887,
Gore, Mrs. Wm., 1887,

Graves, Walter R. (Student), 1891
Gregory, Judge Jno. M., 1884,
Gregory, Mrs. Jno. M., 1884,
Gregory, Miss Letty, 1884,
Hall, Dr. J. Lesslie, 1889,
*Hall, Mrs. J. Lesslie, 1890,
Halstead, Miss Q. N., 1871,
Hancock, Mrs. Clarissa, 1868,
Hancock, Miss Sophia, 1868,
Hankins, Miss Alice, 1868,
Hankins, Mr. Geo., 1868,
*Hankins, Mrs. Geo., 1868,
*Hankins, Miss Harriet (M. Richardson†), 1868,
*Hankins, Miss Harriet Parker, 1903,
Hankins, Reynolds, 1899,
Hansford, Mr. Chas., 1887,
*Harrison, Miss Louise, 1903,
Harrison, Coll. Randolph, 1870,
*Harrison, Mrs. Randolph, 1870,
*Harrison, Randolph, 1902,
Hauley, Mrs., 1868,
Hazlegrove, Mr., 1868,
Hazlegrove, Mrs., 1868,
*Henley, Miss Bettie, 1885,
*Henley, Miss Catharine N., 1898,
Henley, Mrs. Harriet, 1868,
*Henley, Miss Ida G., 1898,
Henley, Miss Janie W., 1892,
*Henley, Leonard, 1887,
*Henley, Mrs. Norvelle L., 1898,
*Hensley, Miss Emily Marianne, 1900,
Hensley, Miss Florence G. (M. Baron de Launay†), 1900,
Herbert, Thomas S. (Student), 1893,
Hinton, Coll. Peter, 1884,
Hobson, A. G. W., 1871,
Hobson, Mr. Canon (Student), 1871,
Holston, A. W. (Student), 1894,
*Hoy, Dr. W. P., 1899,

List of Communicants from 1868 to 1904

*Hughes, Sidney S. (Student), 1903,
Humphreys, Harry G. (Student), 1904,
*Hundley, A. E., 1887,
Hundley, H. L., 1887,
*Hundley, Mrs. M. Brooks, 1891,
*Hundley, Miss Sue D., 1902,
Hunnicutt, Miss Lizzie, 1868,
Hurt, Mrs. Mary, 1868,
*Jackson, Miss Lelia, (M. Durfey†) 1871,
*Johnston, Mr. W. C., 1894,
Jones, Mr. Henley T., 1868,
Jones, Mrs. H. T., 1868,
Jones, Hugh W., 1893,
*Jones, Miss Marian A. (M. Stone†), 1891,
Jones, Mr. Wm., 1883,
Kincheloe, Edw. R. (Stu.), 1892,
*Knight, Jno. W., 1904,
*Knight, Mrs. Jno. W., 1904,
Lacy, Mr. T. S., 1871,
*Lamb, Miss Bessie, 1903,
Lamb, Mrs. Harriet, 1868,
*Lamb, Junius B, 1903,
*Lamb, Mrs. Kate (Branch††),1903
*Lane, Miss Carrie D. (M. Cole†), 1885,
Lane, Miss Cora (M. Denmeade†), 1891,
*Lane, Capt. L. W., Sr., 1904,
Lane, L. W., Jr., 1887,
*Lane, Mrs. L. W., Sr., 1888,
*Lane, Spencer, 1894,
Langhorne, Mr., 1869,
Langhorne, Mrs., 1869,
Lawrence, N. T., 1904,
Lea, Coll. John, 1868,
Lea, Mrs. Margaret D., 1868,
Lee, Miss Petticolas (M. Powell†), 1891,
*Lightfoot, Herbert C., 1904,
Lively, Mrs. E. H., 1871,

Lively, Miss I. (M. Bowery†), 1869
*Macon, Mr. W. H., 1894,
*Macon, Mrs. Mary G., 1894,
Maupin, Catherine G., 1891,
Maupin, Miss Virginia E., 1891,
Maupin, Miss Sarah (M. Bidgood†), 1868,
McCandlish, Mrs. M., 1868,
McCandlish, Miss Mary, 1871,
McCandlish, Robt. N., 1887,
McCaw, Jas. B., 1891,
*Meade, Jos. W. (Student), 1903,
Mercer, Corbin, 1878,
Mercer, Miss I. S. W., 1871,
*Mercer, Miss Jean, 1891,
*Mercer, Mr. Jno. L., 1871,
Mercer, Miss Kate, 1868,
Mercer, Mrs. Mary C., 1868,
*Mercer, Miss Mary W., 1894,
Mercer, Mr. Robt., 1871.
Miller, Chas. D. (Student), 1903,
*Moncure, Mrs. Blanch T., 1891,
Moncure, Gabriella B., 1891,
Moncure, Dr. J. D., 1887,
*Morecock, Miss Elizabeth A., 1891,
*Morecock, Miss Kathryne, 1894,
*Morecock, Miss Mary A., 1891,
*Morecock, Mrs. Virginia M., 1870
Morecock, Miss Virginia, 1898,
Morris, Mr. Chas., 1871,
Morris, Miss Louisa G., 1871,
Morris, Miss Mary, 1868,
Morris, Mrs. W. L., 1868,
Morrison, Miss Emily, 1868,
Motley, Mr. John, 1870,
Motley, Mrs. John, 1868,
Munford, Col. John, 1868,
Munford, Mrs. John D., 1868,
Munford, Miss Maria, 1868,
Munford, Miss Nanny (M. Bright†), 1868,
Munford, Miss Sally (M. Coles†), 1868,

Munier, Mr., 1870,
*Neale, Mrs. Mary E., 1871,
Nelson, Miss Sally B., 1868,
*Nimmo, Miss Otelia, 1868,
*O'Keeffe, Francis C., 1903,
*O'Keeffe, Miss Georgia T., 1903,
*O'Keeffe, Mrs. Ida T. E., 1903,
Peachy, B. D., Sr., 1887,
*Peachy, Mrs. Bathurst D., 1903,
Peachy, Miss Betty, 1868,
Peachy, Miss Mittie (M. Wise†), 1870,
*Peachy, Miss Sallie (M. Spencer†), 1868,
Petticolas, Dr. A. E., 1868,
Petticolas, Mrs. A. E., 1868,
*Phillips, Mrs. H. N., 1897,
Pettitt, Mrs., 1868,
Pettitt, Miss Louisa, 1868,
Pierce, Mrs. Rebecca, 1868,
Richardson, Dabney, 1891,
Riddick, Sam'l A. (Student), 1893,
*Roberts, Mr. Lloyd Wynn, 1901,
*Roberts, Mrs. Lloyd Wynn, 1901,
Roberts, Mrs. Wm. T., 1894,
*Rose, Mrs. Elizabeth T., 1889,
*Ruffin, Mrs. Edmund, 1903,
Saunders, Miss Page, 1868,
Saunders, Mrs. Robt., 1868,
*Savage, F. R., 1903,
Savage, Mrs. T. L., 1868,
Scott, Mr., 1870,
*Scott, Miss Bessie, 1884,
Scott, Mrs. Elizabeth, 1869,
Shepherd, Mrs. John H., 1893,
*Sherwell, Mrs. Anna H., 1868,
Sherwell, Miss Ann, 1868,
*Sherwell, Miss Eliz. Parks, 1868,
*Sherwell, Miss Mary K., 1868,
Slater, Mrs. Virginia, 1868,
*Smith, A. E., 1887,
*Smith, Miss Alice C., 1871,
*Smith, Miss Cora, 1884,
Smith, Miss L. B., 1871,

*Smith, Miss Edith, 1884,
*Smith, Miss Estelle, 1884,
Smith, Miss Helen, 1871,
Smith, Henry, 1884,
Smith, Julia (colored), 1868,
Smith, Miss Mattie (M. Hughes†), 1870,
Smith, Sidney, 1884,
Smith, Miss Virginia (M. Newbill†), 1871,
Smith, Mrs. Virginia, 1868,
Smith, Mrs. Willard, 1870,
Southall, Evelyn McL., 1891,
Southall, Mr. Francis, 1884,
Southall, Miss H. M., 1868,
Southall, Miss Kate, 1868,
Southall, Miss Lillie, 1885,
Southall, Miss Lizzie (M. Turner†), 1868,
*Southall, Dr. P. T., 1899,
*Southall, Mrs. P. T., 1899,
Southall, Mrs. Virginia, 1884,
Southall, Miss Virginia, 1868,
*Spencer, J. B. C., 1899,
*Spencer, J. Blair, 1899,
*Spencer, Miss Martha, 1898,
*Spencer, Miss Mary B., 1903,
*Spencer, Mrs. Mary, 1887,
*Spencer, Peachy, 1901,
Stephenson, Miss J., 1869,
*Stubbs, Miss Lucy C., 1897,
*Stubbs, Miss Mary M., 1903,
*Stubbs, Thos. J., Jr., 1894,
*Sweeney, Miss Annie (M. Leaver†), 1885,
*Sweeney, Miss Florence, 1895,
*Sweeney, Miss Garnett, 1895,
*Sweeney, Henley, 1895,
*Sweeney, Mr. H. M., 1887,
*Sweeney, Mrs. Ida, 1887,
*Sweeney, Miss Nellie, 1885,
Sweeney, Wilmer, 1894,
*Tabor, Mrs. E. J., 1902,
Taliaferro, Mrs. Bland, 1884,

List of Communicants from 1868 to 1904   163

Taylor, Mrs. N., Sr., 1868,
Taylor, Mrs., 1868,
Taylor, Mrs. Nathaniel, Jr., 1868,
Taylor, F. Suthgate (Student), 1894,
Taylor, Tazwell (Student), 1891,
Thomas, Upton B. (Student), 1892
Thompson, Miss Julia, 1868,
Thompson, P. Montague, 1891,
Tiernon, Jno. L. (Student), 1893,
Tucker, Mr. Robt. H. (Student), 1892,
Tucker, St. Geo. (Student), 1893,
Tucker, Thomas, 1870,
Tucker, Mrs. Thomas, 1870,
Turner, Mr. J. W., 1870,
Turner, Mr. Thurston, 1871,
*Tyler, Mrs. Annie (Tucker††), 1889
*Tyler, Miss Elizabeth G., 1902,
*Tyler, Miss Julia G., 1897,
Tyler, Harry T. (Student), 1891,
Vanneison, Mr., 1871,
Vaughan, Mrs. Bessie, 1869,
Vest, Mrs. Mary, 1868,
Vest, Miss Willie, 1868,
Waller, Maj. H. M., 1885,
Waller, John, 1869,
Waller, Mrs. Julia, 1868,
Waller, Miss Kate Page (M. Langhorne†), 1868,
Waller, Mrs. Nanny, 1868,

Waller, Mr. Robt. Page, 1868,
*Warburton, Miss Letty, 1887,
Ware, Mrs., 1871,
Warren, Mrs., 1868,
*Webb, Miss Susan G., 1894,
Weinberger, Mrs., 1868,
Weymouth, John (Student), 1891,
*Wharton, Miss Alice, 1903,
Wilburn, Miss G., 1871,
Wilburn, Mr. E. D., 1870,
Wilburn, Mrs. Sarah, 1871,
*Wilkins, Miss Hattie A., 1891,
Wilkinson, Miss, 1868.
Wilkinson, Mr. Cary, 1868,
Wilkinson, Mrs. Cary, 1870,
Wilkinson, Miss Willie, 1868,
Wilkinson, Miss Virginia, 1871,
Williams, Mrs. L. W., 1887,
Williams, Miss Eleanor, 1892,
Williams, Miss Elizabeth, 1892,
Williams, Miss Mary H., 1892,
Williamson, Mrs. Mary, 1868,
Wilmer, Mrs. Geo. T., 1870,
Wilmer, Miss Annie, 1870,
Wilmer, Geo. T., D. D., 1870,
Wilmer, Miss Mary, 1870,
Wills, Jas. Henry (Student), 1892,
*Wise, Miss Jennie, 1894,
Wooten, Miss Delia A. C., 1885,
*Wright, Arthur D. (Student), 1903.

Meeting of the Advisory Committee on the Restoration of Bruton Church

On Thursday morning, February 25th, 1904, a meeting of the Advisory Committee on the Restoration of Bruton Church was held in the Church at 11 o'clock, Rt. Rev. A. M. Randolph, D. D., LL. D., Rev. B. D. Tucker, D. D., and Rev. J. J. Gravatt, of the Advisory Committee, were present. Divine service was said in the Church at eleven o'clock by the Bishop of the Diocese, assisted by the Rector of the Church. Immediately after the service the members of the Advisory Committee above mentioned, with Dr. Van F. Garrett, S. W., Mr. H. D. Cole, Register, Mr. John L. Mercer and Dr. L. S. Foster, members of the Vestry, met in the North Transcept of the Church. The Rector, Rev. W. A. R. Goodwin, introduced Mr. J. Stewart Barney, Architect, of New York City, and stated that Mr. Barney, who was a Virginian by birth, and devoted to the cause of preserving Virginia antiquities, had very kindly and generously offered to prepare plans and specifications for the restoration of Bruton Church to its original form without charge to the Church. Bishop Randolph was called to the chair, and Mr. H. D. Cole, of the Vestry, was appointed secretary of the meeting. The following resolution was then offered by the Bishop, and was unanimously adopted by the Advisory Committee, Rector, and Vestry:

Resolved: First, That the generous offer of Mr. J. Stewart Barney to submit plans and specifications for the restoration of Bruton Church be accepted with the thanks of the vestry, congregation, and the diocese.

The work proposed was then carefully considered and fully discussed. The following resolutions were unanimously adopted by the Advisory Committee, subject to the approval of the Parish Vestry and the Architect:

Resolved: Second, That the Architect be requested to restore, as far as possible, the Colonial Governors' pew and the old corner pulpit, with canopy and sounding-board. (Adopted.)

Resolved: Third, That it is the sense of the Advisory Committee that the present partition obstructing the west end of the Church be removed, and the nave restored to its original form. (Adopted.)

Resolved: Fourth, That it is the sense of the Advisory Committee that the gallery in the east end of the Church be removed unless it be found that it belonged to the original form of the Church. (Adopted.)

Resolved: Fifth, That the Architect be advised to restore the aisles to their former condition in so far as in his judgment it may be necessary for the restoration. (Adopted.)

Resolved: Sixth, That it is the sense of the Advisory Committee that the chancel be placed in the east end of the Church. (Adopted.)

There was a decided conviction on the part of all who were present at this meeting that in view of the fact that this Church is more intimately associated than any other in America with the life and history of the Colonial period, it should be faithfully and completely restored to its original form and appearance, in so far as such restoration will not materially unfit the Church for its present and future use in the service of God, for which purpose it was built, and must, primarily, be perpetually devoted.

Ratification by the Parish Vestry

At a meeting of the Parish Vestry held on March 12th, 1904, the resolutions above mentioned were unanimously adopted and ratified. A resolution of the Advisory Committee relative to the restoration of the galleries added to the Church, (see pages 43 and 44) was held in abeyance for further consideration by the Vestry and Architect.

Concluding Note

PRESERVE THE ANTIQUITIES THAT REMAIN!

The assurance that this book will necessarily aid in preserving the contents of the historical records and memorials of a by-gone age guarantees the fulfilment of the prime purpose with which the work was undertaken. What time has forever obliterated, what careless scribes never recorded, what more careless custodians possessed and lost or mutilated of the records of the past, we vainly begrudge.

We trust that this desire for what is lost, and a deeper appreciation of what has been preserved, will stimulate this and succeeding generations to guard and protect and carefully preserve the old Church, and the original records upon paper, and in marble which tell, in the language of our fore-fathers, somewhat of its history.

These memorials of the past are of priceless value, and no cost should be spared to preserve them. Here, and elsewhere in Virginia, are records and memorials which at present are in danger of being destroyed by fire, and which are being injured by handling, and by exposure. Provision should be made for their preservation. Vaults absolutely fire-proof should be built for receiving them. The pages of old record books and parish registers should be covered with silk. Each year adds to their value, but as now preserved and protected each day imperils their very existence.

Even now there are times when restorers and antiquarians would gladly give thousands of dollars for one page of an old vestry book that would bring back an original description of a chancel plan, or tell the exact location of some historic spot. But the page is gone. It was consigned to the care of the mice, or torn out by the parson's boy, or burned, after having been preserved hundreds of years, with the rector's house or the home of a vestryman. We are coming to realize the folly and misfortune of all this. And yet much that remains of the

Concluding Note 167

historic past is still left without safeguard and protection. The custodian of these time-honored memorials holds a sacred trust, and should guard that trust with fidelity. It is possible to arouse a sentiment that will work good results in this direction. There is much that is insecurely preserved in the Episcopal church in Virginia, which will be lamented as forever lost unless this matter receives the attention it deserves.

Name Index

The numbers in parenthesis denote the number of times the name occurs on the page indicated.

Abbott, 117.
Able, 131.
Alcorn, 140.
Aleraft, 141.
Alexander, 124, 141, 158.
Alintof, 139.
Allardis, 137.
Allen, 139 (2).
Ambler, 60, 61, 118, 154, 158.
Amy, 154.
Anderson, 59 (3), 122, 128, 129, 137, 139, 154 (2), 158.
Andrews, 52, 130.
Andros, 18.
Anne, Queen, 69, 76, 88.
Anson, 154.
Archer, 71, 90, 98, 115 (2), 119 (2), 125, 134, 135, 138, 141 (2), etc.
Armistead, 90, 120, 125, 154 (3), 158 (7).
Arnest, 128, 129.
Atherton, 125.
Atkins, 122, 123, 124.
Atwood, 135, 136, 141.
Aylett, 12, 14, 119, 134, 135.
Aynscough, 126 (5), 154.

Bag, 141.
Backercet, 140.
Backhurst, 141.
Bacon, 130, 150.
Bainton, 136.
Baker, 131, 140, 154.
Baldridge, 114.
Ball, 42.
Ballard, 119 (2), 134, 136.
Banister, 132.
Barber, 119, 141 (2), 154.
Barden, 122, 123, 142.
Bardett, 154.
Barnes, 126, 128, 133, 134.

Barnet, 115.
Barney, 164.
Barradall, 102, 115, 119, 120, 154.
Barrett, 139, 158.
Bartle, 125.
Bartlett, 138.
Barton, 149 (2).
Bascom, 135.
Baskerfield, 154.
Bassett, 55, 120, 128, 154.
Bates, 134, 135, 136(3), 137, 154.
Batos, 133.
Battaile, 90.
Batten, 132 (2), 137.
Beale, 119, 130.
Beall, 154.
Becker, 158.
Bee, 134, 141.
Bell, 124, 125, 126, 127, 128, 134, 135 (2).
Bellini, 154.
Bendall, 125, 127.
Bengerfield, 139.
Bentley, 138, 139.
Berkley, 7, 12, 89, 132, 151.
Besouth, 12, 14, 35, 119, 135, 136, 141.
Besser, 154.
Besserer, 131.
Bessy, 134.
Beverly, 7, 15.
Bibb, 158.
Bingham, 116.
Binkfield, 132, 133, 136.
Bird, 125, 158 (2)
Bishop, 158.
Bisit, 134 (2).
Black, 128.
Blackburn, 115.
Blackley, 97, 116.
Blaikley, 142, 154 (2)

Name Index 169

Blair, 26, 27, 28, 29, 30, 31, 33 (2), 36, 37, 38 (3), 39, 43, 51, 80, 106, 107, 108, 115, 116, 118, 119 (2), 122 (2), 123 (2), 126, 127, 142, 154.
Bland, 8, 119, 128.
Blassingham, 127, 130.
Bloxton, 158 (3).
Blouette, 140.
Bocock, 154.
Bolling, 32 (2).
Bolton, 126, 130, 140.
Bond, 126, 127, 128, 129.
Bonyman, 15, 41, 137 (4), 138, 140.
Booker, 130, 154.
Booth, 120, 158 (7).
Bowcock, 154.
Bowers, 59.
Bowery, 158, (2).
Bowman, 158 (2).
Boyden, 132, 158.
Bracken, 48, 49, 51, 52, 69, 118, 130 (2), 131.
Bradford, 123.
Bradley, 127.
Braithwaite, 158 (7).
Brand, 135.
Branch, 158 (2).
Bray, 12, 42, 86, 108, 109, 110, 116 (5), 119 (5), 131, 134, 136 (2), 139, 140 (3), 154 (3).
Brewer, 137.
Bridgers, 135, 142.
Bridson, 140.
Briggs, 116 (2).
Bright, 59, 120, 158 (6).
Bristow, 130, 131.
Broad, 135.
Broadbank, 139.
Brock, quoted, 87.
Bromfield, 132 (2).
Brook, 141.
Brookman, 137.

Brooks, 137, 158, 159 (2).
Brower, 120, 135, 138, 159 (2).
Brown, 104, 107, 116, 123, 124, 125, 128, 129 (2), 154 (3), 159 (2)
Browne, 59.
Brownell, 159.
Bryan, 40, 119, 123, 125 (2), 126 (2), 128, 129, 141 (2), 154 (7).
Bryum, 142.
Buck, quoted, 68, 142.
Bucktrout, 115 (6), 120, 159.
Buffin, 140.
Buford, 154.
Bulger, 141.
Bullifant, 130, 154.
Bullock, 133.
Burch, 61, 62, 118.
Burdett, 154.
Burfoot, 154.
Burgess, 95, 116.
Burke, 159 (4).
Burkey, 135.
Burns, 159.
Burrish, 141.
Burrows, 159.
Burton, 140.
Burum, 142.
Burwell, 29, 38 (2), 40, 59, 115, 119, 120, 123 (2), 154 (7).
Buskey, 159.
Byrd, 42, 88, 122 (2), 123.

Cabaniss, 117, 120.
Cain, 142.
Camm, 118, 159 (8).
Camp, 123, 128 (2), 129, 142, 154 (4).
Campbell, 55, 120, 128, 154 (4).
Carter, 59, 122 (2), 125, 126 (4), 127 (4), 128 (3), 129 (3), 130, (2), 154 (7).
Cary, 33, 59, 114, 119, 140 (2), 159 (2).

Casement, 136.
Casey, 138.
Casper, 115.
Chapman, 155.
Charlton, 94, 116, 128, 155 (2).
Chesley, 12, 119, 134.
Chichester, 159.
Chiswell, 80, 155 (2).
Chowning, 126, 155.
Christian, 59, 60, 120 (3), 159 (6).
Claiborne, 13, 159 (2).
Clark, 133.
Clarke, 136, 137.
Clay, 39.
Clayton, 119, 129, 137 (2), 142.
Clopton, 120, 159 (3).
Clows, 116.
Clowes, 159.
Coales, 155.
Cobb, 12, 14, 135, (2), 139, 140.
Cobbs, 36, 119 (4), 123, 135, 136, 138 (3), 139, 140, 155 (2).
Cock, 123.
Cocke, 89, 90, 129, 140, 155, 159.
Cogbill, 116.
Coke, 59, 120, 122, 123, 126 (2), 127, 155 (4).
Cole, 55, 59, 60, 61, 64, 120 (4), 126, 128, 131, (2). 133, 135, 140, 159 (5), 164.
Coleman, 59, 60, 115, 116, 120 (2), 139, 152, 159 (7).
Collett, 93, 116.
Colonna, (159).
Colvil, 142,
Coman, 136.
Connilly, 127, 128, 129.
Conrad, 149.
Coutesse, 90, 141.
Cook, 133, 139 (2), 142.
Cooper, 133, 134, 136, 141.
Copeland, 120.
Cordwainer, 137.

Corker, 119, 134.
Corking, 135, 138.
Cornon, 133.
Corville, 136.
Cosby, 122, 140, 141, 155.
Cosnahan, 159 (3).
Cotton, 155.
Coupland, 159 (5).
Couser, 142.
Coulthard, 121, 155.
Cowles, 131.
Crabtree, 133.
Craig, 125, 126, 128.
Craige, 155 (2).
Craton, 127.
Crawford, 114.
Crawley, 18, 20, 119 (2), 125 (2), 130, 155 (6).
Crease, 142, 155.
Crenshaw, 132 (3), 133 (2), 135.
Crisps, 137.
Crocus, 137.
Cromley, 80.
Crone, 128.
Crooke, 135.
Cumbo, 131 (3)
Cunningham, 140.
Curteen, 14 (3).
Curtis, 125.
Custis, 8, 43, 88, 89, 116 (3), 119, 139, 143, 150 (5), 151, 155, (4), 159 (5).
Cutherell, 159 (2).

Daisy, 114.
Dale, 155.
Dandridge, 89.
Daniel, 136.
Daniell, 133.
Dargan, 114.
Darlington, 159 (3).
Davenport, 124 (2), 125 (2), 126, 127 (3), 128, 129, 140 (2), 141 (2), 155 (3).

Name Index

Davis, 96, 123 (2), 124, 132 (6), 133, 135 (2), 136, 137, 138, 139, 140 (2), 141 (4), 159 (3).
Davidson, 143 (2).
Dawson, 37, 38, 39, 44, 118, 155 (4).
Day, 138, 155, 160.
Dean, 130, 140.
Deekens, 120.
Dehart, 116.
Delony, 140.
Dennis, 128, 132, 139.
Dennison, 60, 118, 148.
Desveer, 138.
Dew, 59.
Dewbre, 129.
Dick, 131.
Dickenson, 155 (2).
Dickeson, 135.
Dickinson, 122 (3), 123, 124, 125, 134, 155.
Dickson, 130.
Didip, 125.
Digby, 135.
Digges, 112, 124, 155.
Diggs, 113, 121, 123.
Dinwiddie, 7.
Dix, 116, 160.
Dixon, 116, 120, 129, 155 (3), 160 (2).
Dod, 160 (2).
Dodgson, 160.
Doran, 127.
Dorman, 18, 82.
Dormar, 20, 119, 134.
Dormer, 78.
Douglas, 142.
Dowson, 137.
Doyley, 20, 22(2), 78, 118, 137 (3).
Drake, 136.
Drewitt, 138, 139.
Druitz, 130, 155.
Drumond, 155 (2).
Drummond, 151.

Drysdale, 7.
Dubree, 130, 131.
Dudley, 90.
Duffin, 140.
Dugger, 115.
Dunford, 132.
Dunmore, 7, 43.
Dunn, 124, 127.
Dunston, 139, 140.
Durfey, 59, 60 (2), 61, 117 (3), 120 (2), 122, 123 (5), 126 (2), 129, 133, 134, 146, 160 (2).
Dyer, 106, 116, 138 (2), 139 (3), 140 (3), 141 (2).

Earnshaw, 129.
Eaton, 39, 119, 120, 124, 155 (3).
Eburne, 17, 18, 19, 20, 118, 145.
Edloe, 55, 59, 120 (2), 160.
Edmunds, 142.
Edwards, 134, 160.
Effingham, 18.
Eggleston, 127.
Eldred, 160.
Elwood, 160.
Empie, 54, 56, 118.
English, 155.
Equo, 133.
Esco, 122.
Evans, 120, 132, 135(2), 136, 137, 160.
Evelyn, 88.
Everard, 39, 40, 119, 155.
Everitt, 141.
Ewell, 120, 160.

Falkiner, 160 (2).
Farmer, 138.
Fauquier, 7, 91, 121, 155.
Fear, 129, 135.
Fellows, 135.
Fenn, 13.
Fennock, 140.
Fergusson, 142, 155 (2).

172　　　　　　　　　　　　　　　　　　　　Name Index

Field, 134.
Filpott, 138 (2).
Finnie, 131, 155 (3).
Fisher, 132.
Fitzhugh, 102.
Flax, 130.
Flemming, 50, 142.
Folio, (and 'ot) 132 (2), 142.
Forbar, 141.
Force, 122.
Foster, 120, 160 (5), 164.
Foy, 122.
Frank, 95, 116, 125.
Frederick, 134.
Fry, 122 (2).

Galt, 56, 57, 59 (2), 60 (2), 117, 120 (2), 126, 130 (2), 131 (4), 155, 160 (6).
Gardner, 14, 16, 119, 134, 136, 145.
Garland, 135, 155 (2).
Garrett, 59, 60, 61, 63, 64, 116(6), 120 (3), 149, 160 (8), 164.
Gary, 139.
Gay, 160.
Geady, 122.
Geddy, 127, 155.
George, III, King, 46, 48, 70.
George, 140.
Gibbs, 131, 138.
Gibson, 137.
Gilbert, 135, 139, 140, 155.
Gilbey, 132, 134.
Giles, 122, 136.
Gill, 141.
Gillman, 116.
Gilmer, 122, 155.
Glass, 122, 155.
Glasscock, 136, 140.
Glover, 160.
Godfrey, 129.
Goding, 136.
Gold, 136.
Gooch, 7, 69, 142, 155.

Gooding, 140.
Goodson, 130, 155.
Goodwin, 26, 27, 63, 118, 137, 138, 140, 160, 164.
Gore, 160 (2).
Gorham, 136,
Gough, 155.
Grace, 23, 79, 80, 81.
Grady, 115.
Grammar, 147, 148.
Gravatt, 64, 164.
Gravenor, 135.
Graves, 40, 119 (3), 126, 130-132, 133 (3), 136, 137, 142, 155 (3), 160.
Green, 122, 125, 136, 137, 139, 141, 155.
Greenhow, 98, 105, 116 (3), 126, 155
Green Spring, 151.
Greenwood, 130 (3).
Gregory, 90, 133, 160 (3).
Griffin, 55, 59, 117, 120, 134, 155.
Grinley, 97, 116.
Groymes, 142.
Grymes, 155.
Gun, 155,
Gutteridge, 133.
Gwinn, 135.
Gyles, 135.

Haile, 134.
Hale, 135.
Haley, 135, 137.
Hall, 87, 120, 138, 139, 160 (2).
Halstead, 160.
Hames, 138.
Hammer, 136, 138.
Hammond, 142.
Hancock, 160 (2)
Handy, 135.
Hankins, 142, 160 (6).
Hansel, 122, 123.
Hansford, 59, 61, 78, 82, 84, 85, 86, 90, 119, 120, 138, 156 (3), 160.

Name Index

Harmer, 38, 119, 156.
Harmpield or Harmfield, 123.
Harper, 142.
Harris, 140 (2), 141 (2).
Harrison, 8, 49, 57, 60, 136 (2), 138, 141, 160 (4).
Harrop Parish, 11, 12.
Harwood, 126, 129 (2), 130 (2), 156 (4).
Harvey, 134.
Harvy, 132, 137.
Haskett, 134.
Hauley, 160.
Hawthorne, 132 (2), 133.
Hay, 124, 127, 129, 156 (2).
Hayes, 125.
Haynes, 126, 129 (2).
Haython, 121.
Hazell, 133.
Hazlegrove, 160 (2).
Henderson 107, 116 (7).
Henley, 55, 60, 61, 99, 120 (4), 160 (8).
Hennesse, 128.
Henrikiss, 142.
Henry, 8.
Hensley, 160 (2).
Herbert, 160.
Herd, 135.
Hewbank, 135, 136 (3).
Higgison, 136.
Highland, 121, 127, 128 (2).
Hinton, 160.
Hix, 139.
Hobson, 160 (2).
Hodges, 56, 60, 118, 152.
Hoge, 125 (3).
Holdcraft, 127, 129.
Holden, 121.
Holder, 133 (2).
Holliday, 90.
Holloway, 31, 32 (2), 36, 44, 90, 119, 156.
Holston, 160.

Holt, 38, 119, 122 (2), 123 (2), 126 (3), 142 (2), 156 (3).
Hopkins, 136, 138, 141.
Hord, 116.
Hornsby, 99, 116 (2), 136, 156 (2).
Horrocks, 39 (2), 118, 156.
Horsington, 133 (3).
Horsoon, or Horvoor, 136.
Hortshorne, 136.
Howell, 138.
Hoy, 120, 160.
Hoye, 126.
Hubard, 119, 128 (2), 129, 138, 141, 156 (3).
Hubbard, 139, 156.
Hudson, 134 (2), 137.
Huellin, 136.
Hughes, 124 (2), 39, 156, 161.
Hughs, 133, 156.
Huldston, 140.
Hulett, 123 (4), 156.
Humphreys, 80, 141, 161.
Hundley, 120, 161 (4).
Hunley, 124, 125.
Hunnicutt, 161.
Hunt, 101, 116, 142.
Hunter, 130.
Huntington, 64.
Hurst, 133.
Hurt, 161.
Hutchins, 134.

Ince, 125, 141.
Ingles, 109, 138, 139 (3).
Innis, 131.
Ireland, 133.
Irish, 136.
Iserell, 136.
Ivory, 133, 136.

Jackson, 29, 33, 122, 124, 125, 126, 127, 130, 131, 132, 134, 135 (2), 137, 139, 140 (2), 142, 156 (3), 161.

Name Index

James, 124.
Jameson, 156.
Jamestown, 20, 21, 22, 30, 68, 70, 145, 146, 147, 149, 150, 151.
Jaspar, 124.
Jefferson, 8, 24, 44.
Jeffreys, 135.
Jemart, 138.
Jennings, 7, 18, 20, 26, 28, 31, 32, 33, 34, 85, 119, 136, 141 (2), 145.
Jeph, 132.
Jiggets, 130.
Johnson, 120, 130, 132, 136, 137, 139, 140, 142 (2), 156, 161.
Johnsoune, 141.
Johnston, 131, 120, 161.
Jonathan, 133.
Jones, 12, 14, 15, 16(2), 17(2), 33, 41, 42, 85, 88, 90, 103, 113, 115 (2), 116, 117, 118, 119 (3), 120, 123, 125 (3), 130, 133, 134, 135, 136 (2), 137, 138, 139 (2), 142, 156, 161 (5).
Jorgles, 142.
Juce, 138.
Jude, 122 (2), 137.
Juxton, 135.

Kains, 141.
Keating, 115.
Keele, 156.
Keen, 136 (2).
Keith, 52, 118, 122, 156.
Kemp, 156.
Kempe, 105 (2), 117, 132, 133.
Kendall, 18, 20, 35, 119 (2), 137, 156,
Kene, 156.
Kennedy, 140, 156.
Kerle, 135, 137.
Kernochan, 64.
Kerr, 142.
Kincheloe, 161.

King, 133.
Knight, 161 (2).

Lacy, 161.
LaFayette, 57.
Lafoug, 126, 128.
Lamb, 161 (4).
Lancaster, 133.
Lane, 120, 123, 128, 156, 161 (6).
Lang, 142.
Langhorne, 161 (2).
Lano, 128.
Laprade, 141 (2).
Lark, 130 (2).
Larke, 156.
Laughlin, 90.
Laughton, 140.
Lawrence, 161.
Lawson, 156.
Layton, 139.
Lea, 161 (2).
Leaver, 139.
Lee, 8, 161.
Le Merchant, 141.
Lenox, 127 (2), 128, 129.
Leppers, 142.
Lett, 115.
Levie, 142.
Lewis, 140 (2), 142, 156.
Lightfoot, 140, 161.
Limb, 135.
Lindsay 116 (3).
Lisle, 130.
Lively, 161 (2).
Long, 156.
Lord, 138 (2).
Low, 90.
Lounsdale, 135.
Love, 138.
Lucas, 139.
Luckey, 132.
Luckin, 111.
Ludbrook, 136.

Name Index

Ludwell, 7, 12 (3), 13, 15 (2), 18 (2), 20, 23, 38, 42 (2), 78, 80, 81, 82, 83, 84 (3), 85, 104, 105, 116, 119 (3), 134.
Luke, 141.
Lunsford, 105, 117.
Lyndrick, 139.
Lynne, 143, 156.
Lyon, 131.

Macon, 14, 89, 119, 120, 161 (2).
Macgrigor, 142.
Madison, 49, 50, 51.
Maeplin, 124.
Major, 156.
Man, 138.
Mann, 86.
Manly, 137.
Maples, 121, 142.
Marable, 14, 15 (2).
Marsh, 134 (2).
Marshal, 8, 44, 125.
Marston Parish, 11, 12.
Martin, 15, 59, 119, 129, 132, 135, 136, 137, 138, 139 (3).
Martyr, 128.
Marye, 96.
Mason, 8.
Massey, 138.
Masterson, 138.
Mathews, 119, 133 (2), 134 (2).
Matthews, 18 (2), 36.
Maupin, 120, 127, 142 (2), 156 (2), 161 (3).
Maury, 131.
May, 129, 156.
Maynard, 122, 124 (2), 125, 156.
McCandlish, 55, 59, 60, 120, 152, 161 (3).
McCann, 116.
McCarty, 140 (2), 156 (4).
McCaw, 161.
McCloud, 138.
McClurg, 156.

McGrigor, 140.
McIntosh, 122.
McKenzie, 121, 123, 124, 142, 156.
McKim, 64.
McKlim, 124.
McPherson, 131.
Meade, 51, 161.
Mecarte, 137.
Mecharte, 138.
Meeke, 135.
Menetree, 140.
Mercer, 49, 63, 120 (2), 161 (8), 164.
Meredith, 61, 118.
Merriwether, 32 (2).
Metcalf, 156.
Middlesex Parish, 11.
Mille, 135.
Miller, 59, 135, 161.
Millington, 59, 115, 120, 141 (2).
Mills, 136 (2), 137.
Milton, 133.
Minitree, 138, 139.
Minnis, 130.
Mires, 127.
Mitchell, 126, 138.
Moodley, 141.
Moody, 126, 128, 129, 130, 156 (4).
Mooney, 115.
Moore, 51, 55.
Moncure, 120, 161 (3).
Monroe, 8, 44.
Montgomery, 90.
Moor, 140.
More, 114.
Morecock, 120, 161 (5).
Moreland, 142.
Morgan, 133, 140.
Moring, 124.
Morris, 34, 139, 161 (4).
Morrison, 68, 117, 148, 161.
Morrow, 124.
Morton, 129 (4), 131, 156.
Moss, 156.

Mottley, 161 (2).
Moyer, 127, 156.
Mouring, 139.
Mourning, 122.
Munford, 61, 120, 161 (5).
Mundell, 142, 156.
Munier, 161.
Munroe, 140.
Murpha, 141.
Musgrove, 123, 124.

Neale, 162.
Needler, 119.
Nelson, 131, 156.
Newitt, 156 (2), 162.
Newman, 141.
Newton, 137, 142.
Nicholas, 7, 39 (2), 40, 119 (2), 128 (2), 129, 141, 142, 143, 156.
Nichols, 123, 136.
Nicholson, 7, 20, 22, 25, 77, 78, 80, 81, 84, 156 (3).
Nicolson, 94, 100, 116, 117, 124(2), 125 (2), 127, 128, 130, 138.
Ninino, or Nimno, 142, 162.
Normand, 123.
Northy, 76, 77, 83, 84.
Norwell, 18, 20, 29, 78, 82, 84, 85, 140, spelled Norvell, 119, 135.
Nott, Gov., 26, 100, 117, 138.

Oates, 124 (2), 125.
Obrian, 140.
O'Connor, 142.
Ogleby, 141.
O'Keeffe, 162 (3).
Ormi(or e)ston, 126 (2).
Orr, 93, 116, 156.
Orrell, 130
Overby, 61, 118.
Owen, 135 (3).
Owens, 12, 20, 119, 137, 145.

Owman, 140.
Oxley, 135.

Pack, 141 (2).
Packard, 148.
Page, 7, 12, 13 (2), 14, 15, 16 (2), 41, 42 (3), 55, 57, 59, 61, 71, 77, 82, 84, 85, 86, 111 (4), 112 (2), 113 (2), 116(5), 118, 119(3), 120, 122, 123, 136 (5), 137, 145, 156 (2).
Paget, 140.
Palmer, 120, 156.
Paradice, 156.
Parke, 7, 12 (2), 13, 18, 20, 88, 119 (2), 132 (2), 134, 137, 138, 150 (2).
Parker, 156.
Parks, 120, 156.
Parr, 114.
Parris, 142.
Parrott, 156.
Partridge, 133, 136.
Pasteur, 126, 129, 141 (4), 156.
Patterson, 156.
Paxton, 26.
Peachy, 55, 59, 61, 120 (4), 122, 162 (5).
Peal, 124.
Peale, 156.
Pearman, 129.
Pearson, 14, 119, 125, 127, 128, 129, 156.
Pegram, 140, 142.
Peirson, 134, 136 (2).
Pelham, 44, 47, 127.
Penbethman, 133, 138.
Pendleton, 8, 50, 149.
Pennele, 142.
Pennman, 124, 142.
Penny, 156.
Peters, 124, 133, 156.
Petticolas 162 (2).
Pettitt, 162 (2).

Name Index

Pettus, 108, 119.
Philip, 132.
Phillips, 127, 129, 133, 136, 162.
Phrodono, 132.
Pierce, 39, 59, 119 (2), 120, 135, 156, 162.
Pilkinton, 120.
Pinchback, 138.
Pi(y)nes, 137 (2).
Pinkethman, 18, 20 (2), 78, 84 (2), 85, 119 (2), 133, 134, 137 (2), 138, 139.
Pitt, 130, 156.
Poindexter, 15, 119.
Pollard, 137, 141.
Porter, 128, 135.
Potter, 156.
Powell, 38, 40, 125 (4), 126 (2), 156.
Power, 38, 120.
Powers, 139.
Pratt, 142.
Predy, 132.
Prentis, 40, 119, 120, 130, 131, 157 (4).
Preston, 136, 137.
Priar, 157.
Prichard, 135.
Prior, 139.
Prosser, 129.
Pulley, 139.
Purdie, 96, 117, 127, 128.
Purdy, 157.

Rae, 94, 117.
Radcliff, 131.
Randal, 157 (2).
Randolph, 7, 8, 36, 38, 39, 44 (3), 49, 50, 52, 59, 64, 115, 119 (2), 120, 121, 157 (3), 164.
Ratcliff, 130 (2), 139, 157.
Ratlift, 129.
Ravenscroft, 136.
Rawley, 123, 143.

Rawlinson, 123.
Reade, 70, 139.
Rector, 115.
Reed, 122.
Reid, 157.
Renolds, 123.
Rentmore, 134.
Reynolds, 127, 131, 142.
Rhodes, 125, 122 (5).
Rhodewell, 142 (2).
Rice, 124, 136.
Richardson, 134, 162.
Richerson, 125.
Ricket, 127.
Riddal, 140.
Riddel, 157.
Riddick, 162.
Rind, 128, 129.
Roadman, 131, 157.
Roan, 136.
Roberts, 62, 118, 123, 127, 136, 157 (2), 162 (3).
Robertson, 25, 26, 42, 77, 85, 119.
Robinson, 123 (2), 124, 134, 135, 136, 157.
Rogers, 120, 134 (2), 135.
Rogerman, 142.
Rollison, 130.
Rose, 125, 128 (2), 162.
Ross, 138.
Rovear, 139.
Row, 138.
Royall, 81.
Royle, 127, 157 (3).
Rudder, 140.
Ruffin, 162.
Russell, 123, 124, 130, 131, 132, 133, 134, 157 (2).

Sadler, 140.
Saint, 134.
Sampson, 134.
Sanders, 129, 137, 141.
Sandford, 130.

Name Index

Sands, 133 (3), 134.
Saunders, 57, 59, 60, 61, 120 (2), 127, 129, 157 (2), 162 (2).
Savage, 116, 162 (2).
Scarborough, 157 (2).
Sclater, 17, 26, 27.
Scot, 130, 134.
Scott, 4, 44, 162 (3).
Scrivener, 98, 116.
Sebrill, 135 (2), 136, 137, 138.
Semple, 55, 120 (2).
Serjeanten, 141.
Sexton, 134.
Sharpe, 133, 139, 140.
Shehorne, 138 (2).
Shelburn, 137.
Sheldon, 59, 120.
Sheppard, 127.
Shepherd, 162.
Sherman, 139.
Sherwell, 162 (4).
Shields, 59, 120, 121, 122, 123, 128, 130, 131, 141, 142, 157 (2).
Shoemaker, 157.
Short, 157.
Shurley, 133.
Sidderdell, 157.
Simpkins, 13, 134 (2).
Simpson, 134.
Simson, 145.
Singleton, 125, 157 (2).
Skaif, 142.
Skinner, 56.
Skipwith, 142.
Slater, 162.
Smith, 115 (2), 117, 120, 139, 140, 157, 162 (14).
Snow, 116.
Somorton, 133.
Southall, 59, 120 (2), 126, 127 (2), 128, 157 (2), 162 (10).
Southgate, 117.
Sparrow, 148.
Spelman, 137.

Spence, 142.
Spencer, 120 (2), 162 (6).
Spottswood, Gov., 7, 33 (3), 34, 89
Spratley, 157.
Spring, 14, 119, 135.
Spurr, 39, 157.
Stafford, 137.
Staige, 95, 96.
Stanley, 139.
Stannup, 142.
Stanton, 69.
Stanyard, 136.
Stark, 157.
Stay, 157.
Steel, 157.
Stephens, 133 (2).
Stephenson, 115, 125, 162.
Stevens, 124, 135, 138, 142.
Stevenson, 123.
Stevinson, 157.
Steward, 136, 138, 140.
Stith, 97, 116, 157 (3).
Stokes, 131.
Stone, 124, 126, 132, 141 (2).
Stott, 142, 157.
Stover, 139.
Straughan, 140, 141.
Strawhun, and hawne, 132 (2).
Street, 127, 128, 157.
Strickland, 138.
Stuart, 117.
Stubbs, 162 (3).
Sturgis, 134.
Summers, 135.
Sutor, 136.
Swiney, 157.
Sweeney, 162 (8).
Syms, 139.
Syncock, 138.

Tabor, 162.
Taliaferro, 61, 90, 120, 157, 162.
Tandy, 137.
Tantey, 134.

Name Index

Tarpley, 71, 157 (2).
Tarrent, 140.
Taylor, 14, 26, 59, 90, 119, 120, 122, 126, 129, 134, 135 (2), 136, 139, 140 (2), 141, 142, 143, 157 (2), 163 (5).
Teddar, 135, 137.
Teer, 137 (2)
Temple, 137.
Theological Seminary, Alexandria, 52, 148, 149.
Thomas, 132 (2), 138, 163.
Thompson, 34, 61, 96, 120, 141 (2), 163 (2).
Thornton, 157.
Thorp, 71, 101, 102, 116 (2), 119 (2), 134 (2), 136, 137 (2).
Tibbs, 136.
Tiernon, 163.
Tilford, 116.
Tillet, 33.
Tillyard, 26, 27.
Timberleck, 139.
Timson, 82, 84, 85, 119 (2), 120, 124, 129, 135, 137 (2), 138, 140, 142 (2), 143, 157 (3).
Tobin, 140.
Todd, 133.
Todeink, 132.
Tomson, 139 (2).
Toop, 134 (2).
Townsend, 134.
Trebell, 157.
Trewly, 142.
Trower, 127.
Tucker, 50, 59, 64, 115, 117 (2), 120, 133, 163 (4), 164.
Tuley, 132.
Turner, 119, 134, 137, 157, 163 (2).
Twyner, 115.
Tyler, 8, 18, 20, 25, 44, 59, 69, 84, 90, 106, 119, 120, 135, 137, 138 (2), 139 (2), 141 (2), 142 (2), 157, 163 (4).

Vadin, 135 (2).
Valentine, 129, 157.
Vanneison, 163.
Vaulx, 119, 132, 134 (2), 140.
Vaughan, 163.
Veale, 134.
Vest, 59, 60, 61, 120 (2), 163 (2).
Vinkler, 14 (3), 119, 137.
Vobe, 157.

Wade, 121, 126, 139.
Wadsworth, 135.
Wager, 141.
Walker, 60, 120 (2), 132.
Wall, 61, 118, 120.
Wallace, 26, 120.
Waller, 38, 40, 44 (2), 55, 59 (2), 60, 119, 120 (3), 123, 124 (2), 125, 127 (3), 129, 157, 163 (6).
Walters, 132, 135, 157.
Walthorne, 133.
Warburton, 120, 163.
Ward, 124.
Ware, 163.
Warren, 138, 163.
Warrington, 126 (2), 127 (2), 129.
Warters, 157.
Washington, Gen. Geo., 8, 48, 89, 121, 150, 157.
Washington, 50, 90, 115, 150.
Watkins, 124.
Watson, 136, 137.
Wattles, 134 (2).
Weatherburn, 157 (3).
Webb, 55, 120, 138, 163.
Weinberger, 163.
Weldon, 140.
Wellings, 123.
Wells, 122 (2), 132 (2), 133, 136, 137, 138.
West, 136, 138, 140 (2).
Westmore, 127.
Westwood, 116.
Wetherford, 138.

180 Name Index

Weymouth, 163.
Whaley, 110, 116(2), 119(2), 133, 138.
Wharton, 61, 84, 118, 134, 139, 163.
Wheatley, or Whateley, 22(2), 23, 26, 27, 76, 78(4), 80, 82(2), 83, 84, 85 (2), 86(4), 118, 139, 157.
Wheeler, 133.
Whitaker, 157.
Whitby, 137.
White, 78, 82, 86, 119, 128, 129, 132 (3), 133 (2), 135, 136, 137 (3), 138 (2), 139, 141.
Whitehair, 133.
Whitehead, 141.
Whiting, 135, 136.
Whitlock, 139.
Whittaker, 128.
Wickham, 50, 137.
Wiggs, 138 (2).
Wilburn, 163 (3).
Wilkins, 123, 124 (2), 132, 163.
Wilkinson, 133, 134 (2), 135, 141 (2), 163 (5).
William and Mary College, 30, 37, 43, 44, 47, 52, 84, 90, 100, 157.
Williams, 89, 116, 119, 134, 136, 140, 163 (4).
Williamson, 163.

Willis, 141, 157.
Wills, 163.
Wilmer, 52, 53 (2), 60, 61, 62, 91, 116, 118 (2), 147, 149, 163 (4.)
Wilson, 124 (3), 129, 132.
Winchcom, 135.
Winder, 116.
Windsor, 140.
Wingfield, 120.
Wisdem, 134.
Wise, 120, 163.
Withers, 125.
Wolley, 114.
Wood, 142.
Woods, 133 (2).
Woodbridge, 95.
Woody, 157.
Wooten, 163.
Wray, 38, 119, 123 (2), 142, 157 (2).
Wright, 115, 124, 130(2), 131, 163
Wyatt, 116, 122, 142.
Wylde, 119, 132 (2), 134.
Wynn, 141.
Wythe, 8, 39, 40, 44, 48, 50, 119, 157 (2).

Yates, 39, 118, 136, 157.
Young, 141.
Yuille, 93, 116.

Subject Index

Addenda, Historical, including :—
(1) Additional notes from Vestry book of 1674, pp. 145-146. (2) Notes relative to the removal and return of the Jamestown Communion Silver, pp. 147-150. (3) Inscriptions on Custis' tombstones, p. 150. (4) Note relative to scattered and neglected tombstones, p. 151. (5) Note relative to slave baptisms, p. 152. (6) List of persons who had slaves baptized, pp. 154-157. (7) Communicant List from 1868 to 1904, pp. 158-163. (8) Meeting, and action of Restoration Advisory Committee, p. 164. (9) Note relative to the preservation of Historical records and memorials, p. 166.
Associations connected with Church, 7, 66.
Attendance, compulsory, 41.
Baptism of Slaves, 121, 152-157.
Bell, the Church, 16, 40, 71. Belfry, 16, 39, 40.
Birth Record, from 1739 to 1789, 121-131.
Bishop of London, 27, 36, 45, 81, 82
Blair, Commissary, 27, extracts from his sermons, 72, death of, 37
Blandford Church, Petersburg, Va., inscription on wall of, 21, date of, 21.
Boundary line between Bruton Parish and James City, 145.
Buck, John H., quoted, 68.
Burgesses, House of, donations to Church, 31, 32, 37, 38, 42, appealed to, 145.
Burial in Chancel and in Church, fees for, 42.
Catharine Memorial Society, 62.

Church, Building of 1683, 12, of 1715, 31.
Clock, in Church steeple (thought by President L. G. Tyler to have been formerly in House of Burgesses), 60.
Colonial, Church service described, 45. Governors mentioned, 7. Governor's pew, 42, 57.
Communicants, list of from 1868 to 1904, 158-163.
Communion Silver, Queen Anne, 30, 68, 69. Jamestown and King George III silver described and illustrated, 68-70. Protected during the war, 61. Jamestown set removed and restored, 147-150.
Confederate memorial, 92, 114.
Consecration of Church, question of, 16, 51.
Cost of material and labor in 1713, 35.
Death record from 1662 to 1751, 132-143.
Dedication of Church of 1683, 15.
Despoliation, legislative, 49-51.
Dimensions of Church, 32, 33, 34, 37, 38.
Donations to Church, of money, 13, 14, 15, 25, 55, 56. Silver server, 18. Altar Cloth, 25. By House of Burgesses, 32, 33, 38. Legacy from Mrs. Besouth, 35. Bible given, 36. Gift of Church yard land, 42. Furniture by Catharine Memorial Society, 62. Communion Silver, 68-70. Bell, 71. Plans, 33, 164.
Endowment for preservation of Church, should be provided, 67.
Enlargement of Church, 37, 38—.
Episcopal Visitations, 51.

182 Subject Index

Epitaphs and Inscriptions, 87-115, 150.
Fees of Clerk and Sexton, 16.
Fiske, John, quoted, 24.
Font, Jamestown, 22, 70. Illustration of, 30.
Galleries mentioned, 43, 44, 47, 55, 56, 59 (diagram), 60, 62—.
Glebe lands, 36, 49-51.
Governors, Colonial, mentioned, 7. Pew of, 7, 42, 47, 57.
Hall, Dr. J. L., quoted, 87.
Hospital, Church used as, 61.
Induction Controversy, 17, 19, 23, 32, 76-86.
In Memoriam, 67.
Innovations, 55, 56, 62.
Jamestown, abandoned, 20-22, Font, 22, 70. Communion silver, 22, 68, 70, 147-150. Church tower, picture of, 21. Church door, 146. Dispute as to boundary of Parish, 145.
King George, silver, 70.
Mayor's pew, 57.
Middle Plantation, 11, 12, 146.
Ministers, character of, 20, 45. List of, 118. Others mentioned, 26, 49, 64, 123, 130, 137 (2), 141, 142. Salary of, 41.
Name Index, 168-180.
Names of those who had slaves baptized, 154-157.
Names of Pew-renters in 1840, 59.
Names on Tomb-stones, list of, 115.
Names of Vestrymen, 119-120.
Old Regime, passing of, 45.
Organ, secured, 37, loft, 44, sold, 56.
Parish, Formation of, 11, 12. Name of, 12. Limits of, 36. Bounds, dispute as to, 145. Processioned, 146.

Parish House, deeded, 62.
Pews, new ones secured, 36. Oiled, 37. Assigned to Governor, 42, 57. In Chancel, 41, 42. Other pews assigned, 43. Assigned to College students, 43, 44. Cut down, 55. Rented, names of renters, 59. Made free, 60.
Plan of Church of 1715 furnished by Gov. Alex. Spottswood, 33—.
Preservation of tomb-stones, 151. Of old records and memorials, 166.
Presidents who worshipped in Church, 8.
Processioning of Parish bounds, 146.
Pulpit, 36, 62.
Quakers, in arrears, 19, 20.
Record books of Parish, 4, 62, 71. Photograph of, 121. Preservation of, 166.
Repairs to Church mentioned, 19, 22, 25, 35, 36, 37, 52, 62, 67. To tomb-stones, 62.
Restoration movement, 9, 63. Advisory Committee Meeting, 164.
Revolution, effect upon Church, 45, 48. The Church after, 49.
Silver given, 18, 35, 68.
Slaves baptized, the record of, 121. Note as to, 152. Total number each year, 153. Alphabetical list of persons who had slaves baptized from 1746 to 1797, 155-157.
Statistics of Congregation in 1724, 36. In 1821 and 1826, 52. In 1828, 54.
Subscribers to Church Building of 1683, 13-14.
Thomas, R. S., quoted, 49.

Subject Index

Tomb-stone Inscriptions, 87-115. Repaired, 62. Preservation of, 151

Tyler, President Lyon G., quoted, 13, 38, 42, 69.

Universalist minister not allowed to preach in Church, 56.

Vestry, old orders, 41. Book of 1827, 55.

Vestrymen, position and authority of Colonial, 24. Last before Civil War, 60. First after, 61. List of, 119-120.

William and Mary College, 30, 37, 43, 44, 47, 52, 84, 90, 100, 157.

Yard to Church, given, 14, 42. Wall of, 39.

www.ingramcontent.com/pod-product-compliance
Lightning Source LLC
Chambersburg PA
CBHW051738230426
43670CB00012B/2075